WARRIOR 183

BRITISH TANK CREWMAN 1939–45

NEIL GRANT　　ILLUSTRATED BY GRAHAM TURNER

Series editor Marcus Cowper

OSPREY PUBLISHING
Bloomsbury Publishing Plc

Kemp House, Chawley Park, Cumnor Hill, Oxford OX2 9PH, UK
29 Earlsfort Terrace, Dublin 2, Ireland
1385 Broadway, 5th Floor, New York, NY 10018, USA
Email: info@ospreypublishing.com
www.ospreypublishing.com

OSPREY is a trademark of Osprey Publishing Ltd

First published in Great Britain in 2017
Transferred to digital print on demand in 2024

© Osprey Publishing Ltd, 2017

All rights reserved. No part of this publication may be reproduced or transmitted in any form or by any means, electronic or mechanical, including photocopying, recording, or any information storage or retrieval system, without prior permission in writing from the publishers.

A catalogue record for this book is available from the British Library.

Print ISBN: 978 1 4728 1696 2
ePub: 978 1 4728 1698 6
ePDF: 978 1 4728 1697 9
XML 978 1 4728 2486 8

Index by Alison Worthington
Typeset in Myriad Pro and Sabon
Page layouts by PDQ Digital Media Solutions, Bungay, UK
Printed and Bound by Intellicor, LLC USA.

The Woodland Trust
Osprey Publishing supports the Woodland Trust, the UK's leading woodland conservation charity.

www.ospreypublishing.com
To find out more about our authors and books visit our website. Here you will find extracts, author interviews, details of forthcoming events and the option to sign-up for our newsletter.

DEDICATION
For my beautiful wife Kirsty, who has been remarkably accepting of me babbling endlessly about tanks while writing this.

ARTIST'S NOTE
Readers may care to note that the original paintings from which the colour plates in this book were prepared are available for private sale. All reproduction copyright whatsoever is retained by the Publishers. Readers are directed to the following website for further information:

www.studio88.co.uk

The Publishers regret that they can enter into no correspondence upon this matter.

Imperial War Museums Collections
Many of the photos in this book come from the huge collections of IWM (Imperial War Museums) which cover all aspects of conflict involving Britain and the Commonwealth since the start of the twentieth century. These rich resources are available online to search, browse and buy at www.iwm.org.uk/collections. In addition to Collections Online, you can visit the Visitor Rooms where you can explore over 8 million photographs, thousands of hours of moving images, the largest sound archive of its kind in the world, thousands of diaries and letters written by people in wartime, and a huge reference library. To make an appointment, call (020) 7416 5320, or e-mail mail@iwm.org.uk

Imperial War Museums www.iwm.org.uk

CONTENTS

INTRODUCTION — 4

CHRONOLOGY — 5

RECRUITMENT AND TRAINING — 7
Recruitment • Training • Promotion • Officer selection and training

CONDITIONS OF SERVICE — 15
Life on camp • Food • Pay • Discipline and punishments

CLOTHING AND UNIFORM — 18

EQUIPMENT AND PERSONAL WEAPONS — 23
Headgear and webbing equipment • Personal weapons

INSIDE THE TANK — 25
Crew positions • Crew communication • Conditions in a tank

UNIT STRUCTURE — 30

A TANK CREW'S DAY — 32
Time out of line

MORALE AND CREW COHESION — 38

BRITISH TANK DESIGN — 41
Tank armament and gunnery

IN COMBAT — 47
Casualties • The fall of France (September 1939–June 1940) • The Desert Campaign – early days (September 1940–February 1941) • The Greek Campaign (March–April 1941) • North Africa – the Germans arrive (March 1941–May 1943) • The Italian Campaign (September 1943–May 1945) • From Normandy to VE Day (June 1944–May 1945) • The Far East (December 1941–August 1945)

RETURN TO CIVILIAN LIFE — 62

MUSEUMS AND RE-ENACTMENT — 62

BIBLIOGRAPHY AND FURTHER READING — 63

INDEX — 64

BRITISH TANK CREWMAN 1939–45

INTRODUCTION

I saw a Panzer Mark III lumber over the top … my first shot was just short but my second was a direct hit. I slammed in three more for good measure and the turret flaps opened and out jumped the crew. I then switched to Besa machine-gun fire and fired as they tried to get back over the crest and two of them dropped and remained still. This may seem very callous now but at that time it was different entirely. Our crews were being shot at when they bailed out so it seemed entirely and perfectly justifiable to me to do the same to the Jerry crews. (Hamilton 1995, p.21)

Britain produced the first tanks during the Great War (1914–18) to break the stalemate of trench warfare. Although the Tank Corps – renamed the Royal Tank Corps in 1923 and the Royal Tank Regiment in 1939 – was significantly reduced after the Great War ended, Britain maintained a lead in armoured warfare well into the 1920s.

The 'Experimental Mechanized Force' (1927–29) combined a battalion of tanks with armoured cars, mechanized infantry and artillery. This

The crew of a Churchill Mk II tank examine a map during an exercise in October 1942, wearing denim tank suits over battledress. The Churchill had teething troubles after its rushed introduction, but eventually became a well-regarded vehicle. (© IWM TR 211)

performed well against conventional forces in several large exercises, and attracted a good deal of attention, including – ironically – from Germany. However, it was disbanded during severe 1930s defence cuts.

By the late 1930s, war with Germany looked inevitable and Britain began to rearm. It was obvious that a large and effective tank force would be crucial in the coming war. This became the Royal Armoured Corps, including both the Royal Tank Regiment and the newly mechanized Cavalry and Yeomanry regiments.

Simply recruiting and training a tank force which increased ten-fold in size was difficult in itself. However, British tank crews faced additional problems, as British tank design in the early war years left much to be desired.

Over six years of war, British armoured crews fought in the scorching heat of the desert, the mountains of Italy, the dense Normandy bocage and the jungles of Burma.

Infantry might envy tanks their armoured protection, but crews found their vehicles' limited visibility and inability to use cover from enemy fire sometimes made them shockingly vulnerable, and tanks could become blazing steel coffins from which they had only seconds to escape.

Tanks needed careful maintenance even when not in action. After a day of fighting, tank crews had hours of work rearming, refuelling and maintaining their vehicle before they could think about their own needs and getting some sleep before repeating the process the following day.

Britain never produced 'tank aces' in the way that Germany did. Partly, this was a matter of equipment; many high-scoring German 'aces' commanded Tigers, with better firepower and protection than any adversary. It was also a matter of different priorities: Britain's large strategic bomber force meant that some of the best recruits found themselves in Lancaster cockpits instead of tank turrets. There was also a fundamental difference in approach: the Allies believed that numbers and logistics, rather than individual excellence, would determine victory.

This book cannot cover every British tank crewman's experience. Equally, though tank design is discussed, it is ultimately not about the machines, but about the men who fought and sometimes died in them.

CHRONOLOGY

September 1916	First tanks used by Heavy Section, Machine Gun Corps.
July 1917	Heavy Branch MGC renamed the Tank Corps.
May 1927–February 1929	Experimental Mechanized Force.
January 1933	Adolf Hitler becomes Chancellor; German rearmament begins.
September 1938	Munich Agreement cedes Czech territory to Germany. British re-armament begins, but priority goes to RAF and Navy.
April 1939	Royal Armoured Corps formed.
May 1939	Limited conscription introduced.
September 1939	Germany invades Poland. Britain and France declare war. Full conscription begins.

May–June 1940	German forces sweep through Netherlands, Belgium and France. British Expeditionary Force evacuated from Dunkirk, but loses its heavy equipment.
September 1940–February 1941	British repulse Italian invasion of Egypt, but troop transfers to Greece prevent pursuit.
March–April 1941	German Afrika Korps arrives, pushing British troops back to Egyptian border before supply shortage stops them.
April 1941	Germany invades Greece. British troops evacuated, losing their heavy equipment.
June 1941	British mount costly and unsuccessful desert offensive (Operation *Battleaxe*). Germany invades Soviet Union.
July 1941	Lend-Lease tanks begin to arrive in the desert, directly from the US.
September 1941	Last British cavalry regiment (The Royal Scots Greys) mechanized.
November–December 1941	Costly but successful British offensive (Operation *Crusader*) relieves Tobruk and keeps Axis forces out of Egypt.
December 1941	US enters war against Germany and Japan.
December 1941–May 1942	Japanese conquer British possessions in the Far East, including Malaya and Burma.
May–August 1942	British defeat at battle of Gazala. Axis advance stopped at first battle of El Alamein (July) and Alam el Halfa (August).
October–November 1942	Second battle of El Alamein; British return to the offensive, pushing Axis forces out of the western desert.
November 1942–May 1943	Allied landings in Tunisia, encircling Axis forces.
December 1942–May 1943	Unsuccessful British First Arakan offensive in Burma.
September 1943	Allied forces invade Italy but make slow progress.
January 1944–July 1945	Japanese advance towards British India halted at battles of the Admin Box, Imphal and Kohima before Commonwealth forces push Japanese back through Burma.
June–September 1944	Allied landings in Normandy (Operation *Overlord*), followed by heavy fighting to break out of beachhead and push across France.
September 1944	Operation *Market-Garden*. Armoured forces fail to relieve Airborne troops holding Rhine bridge at Arnhem. Operational pause follows, to rebuild supplies.
December 1944–January 1945	Last major German offensive in the Ardennes ('Battle of the Bulge').
March 1945	Allied forces cross the Rhine (Operation *Plunder*).
May 1945	Germany surrenders (VE Day).
June 1945	Demobilization begins.
August 1945	Japan surrenders (VJ Day).

Men of 3 RTR at Warminster, still wearing the pre-war service dress and 1908 pistol belt. Battledress was adopted shortly before the war, and had not become universal by the time of this May 1940 photo. (© IWM H 1545)

RECRUITMENT AND TRAINING

Recruitment

Unlike most European powers, Britain rejected peacetime conscription between the world wars, preferring to rely on a small professional army of volunteers, serving for a minimum of six years with the colours and six in the reserve.

These men often joined in search of travel and excitement, to learn a trade, or simply to escape poverty and unemployment during the 1930s depression. Behind this was a relatively small Territorial Army of volunteer reservists who received military training in their spare time.

It was obvious a larger army would be needed. Britain resisted introducing conscription during the Great War until 1916 but there was no such hesitation this time. The Military Training Act – requiring single men aged between 20 and 22 to undertake six months' compulsory military training – passed in May 1939, three months before war was declared.

This was dramatically extended when war broke out. Parliament immediately passed the National Service (Armed Forces) Act, requiring all males aged between 18 and 41 to register for service.

Men in 'Reserved Occupations' essential to the war effort (including coal miners, farmers, railwaymen, merchant seamen and dockers) were excluded, as were those medically unfit to serve. Conscientious objectors had to appear before tribunals, which might or might not accept their request for non-combatant jobs because of their ethical or religious beliefs.

Conscription was extended to men up to 51 years old and to unmarried women in 1942, though men that old rarely served in combat units.

Men initially registered at the local offices of the Ministry of Labour and National Service, where they gave brief details and could express a preference for serving in the Army, Navy or Air Force. Since not all potential conscripts

The Army centralized general training in 1942, then selected men for advanced training based on aptitude tests. This is recruit Bill Jones taking a mechanical aptitude test in a series of photos that follow him through medical examination, interview and testing before eventual posting to the Royal Tank Regiment. (© IWM H 17185)

could be processed and trained immediately, they then returned home to await the 'call-up papers' summoning them to actual military service.

Once called up, men went to a local recruiting centre, where they received a medical examination and were interviewed briefly by an officer of their preferred service, who recommended where they should be assigned within that service. Future soldiers went directly to their assigned corps or regiment, and received their training there.

Recruits were mostly young – tank commander Rea Leakey noted 'I was the old man of the crew, aged twenty-four' (Leakey 1999, p.28). After the initial rush of conscription ended by 1942, most new recruits joined the Army straight from school.

Overall, the conscripts of 1940 compared favourably with those of 1916. Better diets and public health meant that fewer were rejected on medical grounds, and they averaged almost two inches taller. Most met the 5ft 4in minimum height requirement, though the Guards demanded taller men.

Average education was better, but many technically minded recruits preferred the more glamorous Air Force or Navy. The Army felt it got the poorer recruits, although armoured units received priority for those it did get.

Moreover, the single rather superficial and subjective interview often resulted in skill shortages and men being allocated to jobs for which they were ill suited.

A more scientific system was implemented from 1942. Army recruits (except the Guards) now joined a central 'General Service Corps', where they received six weeks of initial instruction before being put through a battery of tests. These included verbal and mathematical ability, agility, spatial perception and mechanical comprehension, plus a personality test. They were then interviewed by an officer before being allocated to a corps or regiment to complete their training, based largely on the test results.

The new process matched men far more effectively to jobs, improved morale and reduced failure rates in training – that for drivers dropped to 3 per cent, compared to 16–20 per cent under the old system.

Some existing units also converted to tanks en masse. This included the remaining cavalry regiments – the last of which did not mechanize until 1941 – and a number of infantry battalions. In these cases, the men were already trained soldiers and went straight to tank-specific advanced training.

Training

In 1938, new RTC recruits received 24–36 weeks of training at the RTC depot at Bovington in Dorset. This began with administration and kit issue, followed by eight weeks of basic military training, covering drill, turnout, military courtesies, physical training, small arms and map reading.

Since few men learned to drive in civilian life, all recruits received three weeks of driving and maintenance training, followed by six weeks' specialist training in their intended speciality of either driving or gunnery. Often, recruits did both specialist courses, and could perform any task aboard a tank. Finally, all recruits went through four weeks of collective training and exercises, learning tactics and how to handle armour in the field.

This comprehensive training was shortened and simplified once war broke out, as numbers of men to be trained rose enormously. Bovington trained 1,450 recruits in the 1938/39 training year, a considerable increase on the 'peacetime' volumes of previous years. By the height of the war, however, more than 20,000 new tank crewmen were being trained each year.

Wartime recruits initially went directly to one of the RAC training regiments (which specialized in particular types of tanks) for their primary training. This lasted six weeks, covering drill, small arms, military courtesies and so forth. It was followed by another three weeks of general military training, covering camouflage, map reading, basic wireless procedures and driving.

After 1942, primary training was done centrally, with recruits only assigned as tank crewmen after final aptitude testing. This made little difference to the syllabus – which covered skills common to all soldiers – but did result in fewer inappropriate recruits being sent for training as tank crewmen, reducing wastage later in the process.

Wherever recruits received their primary training, they often recalled a tedious and exhausting routine of drill, physical training, kit inspections and being shouted at by NCOs for the smallest infraction in turnout. Most were glad to leave it behind.

Primary training was followed by specialist training in driving, gunnery or signals. Only recruits who were expected to become tank commanders were given any tactical instruction, which caused problems when men were promoted to be commanders in the field.

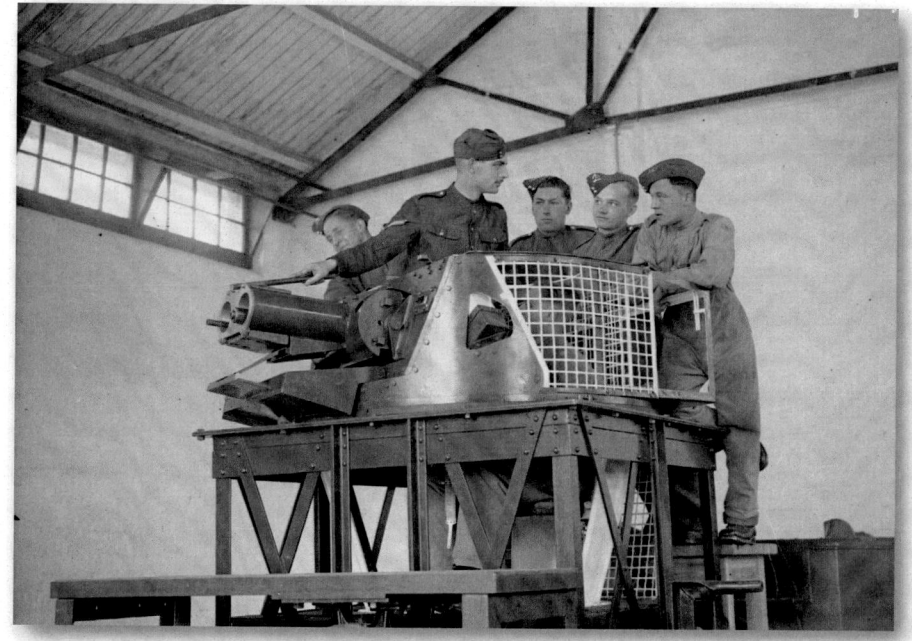

Shortage of vehicles meant much training was done on simulators, like this dual Vickers Gun turret from a Light Tank Mk VI, set up on a small-bore indoor range and used here by men of the 9th Queen's Royal Lancers in the late 1930s. (© IWM Army Training 5/24)

Additional RAC training centres were set up near Cairo, in India and in Italy, so that units could convert to tanks or be trained on new vehicles in theatre.

Training continued in operational units, to build and maintain individual skills and to get crews and troops used to acting together as a team. This was hampered by several factors. During 1940, troops in the UK spent a good deal of time working on fortifications or guarding stretches of coastline against a possible German invasion.

Few tanks were available, so drivers learned on trucks, universal carriers or obsolete light tanks, and training mileage was often restricted to minimize engine wear and conserve fuel.

Main gun ammunition was initially scarce, so gunners spent much of their time practising in mock turrets armed with air guns, firing at miniature tanks being pulled across huge tables set out to represent local countryside with hills, fields and rivers. Michael Halstead recalled in 1940: 'We didn't have much gunnery practice, only three 2-pounder rounds per man, but they gave one the feel of the business at last' (Halstead 1990, p.25).

Each unit might only have a few weeks a year of live firing on the gunnery ranges, mostly against static targets. Units often had to move their tanks considerable distances to use them – 5 RTR was based in Norfolk in 1944, but went to Kirkcudbright in Scotland for gunnery training.

Land for training was at a premium, especially once US forces arrived in preparation for D-day. Several villages around Bovington were evacuated so the area could be used for live fire training, and remain abandoned today.

The U-boat blockade meant all available land was used for agriculture, restricting cross-country movement. These restrictions were relaxed in the run-up to D-day, for obvious reasons – John Foley remembers drivers hesitating when first ordered to drive across fields with standing crops, which they had become used to avoiding.

There were some innovations, such as using training films, but a good deal of time was spent on tedious but necessary camp fatigues (including the infamous 'spud bashing') or things that did not relate to fighting efficiency, such as preparing for showpiece inspections by senior officers or VIPs.

RTR CREWMAN TRAINING IN THE UK, 1940

This RTR crewman is typical of the 1939/40 campaign, with the early concealed button battledress, introduced just before the war. Men were required to wear the shoulder straps of their 1937 webbing, which could be used to lift casualties through vehicle hatches. Fear of gas warfare meant the Small Box Respirator was commonly worn, either slung at the hip or in the 'alert' position on the chest. He carries a 1937 pattern map case, with a rigid board back and pockets on the cover for pencils.

Headgear is the black RAC beret with RTR (**1**) or RAC (**2**) badge, though the British infantry steel helmet (**3**) was also issued. Special tank crew helmets were produced in Britain (**4**) and delivered with US Lend-Lease tanks (**5**) but were little worn. Goggles (**6**) were essential to protect the eyes.

Crews carried .38 Enfield revolvers, both the standard model and a special RAC version without hammer spur (**7**), while each tank came with a Thompson SMG (**8**), stowed with the stock detached, and 6 Mills (No. 36) grenades (**9**). Most also carried an anti-aircraft Bren (**10**).

Personal equipment included identity tags (**11**), 1937 pattern water bottle (**12**), mess tins and enamel mug (**13**) to eat rations which largely consisted of 'M&V', bully beef and biscuit (**14**).

Petrol was initially supplied in 4-gallon cans, known for obvious reasons as 'flimsies' (**15**), though crews scrounged the better-made German Jerrycans (**16**) which were ultimately copied by the Allies. Ammunition for early war British tanks was primarily either 2-pdr (**17**, AP only) or 6-pdr (**18**, AP and HE). Also shown is the RTR shoulder title (**19**).

John Powell (9 RTR) recalled 'fourteen months of simulated battle training which honed our skills ... We didn't learn much about being "under fire" but we became passably good at managing our vehicles, navigating and communicating. And most of the gunners felt confident about hitting a half-way decently presented target' (Beale 1995, p.22).

Promotion

Casualties and enormous expansion of the armoured force brought quick promotion in wartime.

Jock Watt went from being a corporal at the start of the war to RSM and then commissioned before the end of the Desert Campaign, while Bill Close started the war as a sergeant and ended it as a major commanding a squadron.

As newly promoted 3 RTR corporal Geordie Reay remarked: 'It was a simple process of elimination. As long as you survived you would get your promotion. They had to have someone to do the job!' (Delaforce 2010, p.126).

Some soldiers turned down promotion, either because it would mean leaving a good crew where they were happy, or because they didn't want the responsibility of command.

Crusader and Valentine tanks negotiate boggy ground during training in Wales, December 1942. Early Crusader models mounted a small auxiliary machine-gun turret, but this was often left unoccupied in action, and removed from later versions. (© IWM H 26379)

British formations could include men or entire units from the Commonwealth. Here, Sikh Sherman crewmen from the Scinde Horse receive instruction on the Browning machine gun in Iraq, March 1944. (© IWM K 6692)

Officer selection and training

Before the war, British Army officers were drawn from a restricted social pool – 85 per cent of the 1939 intake to the Royal Military Academy, Sandhurst, came from the (fee-paying) public schools, although these educated only 2.5 per cent of boys.

Indeed, Sandhurst itself was fee-paying until 1939 and junior officers' pay was low compared to their peacetime officers' mess subscriptions; it was difficult to become an officer without a private income.

The Army ceased issuing regular commissions with the outbreak of war, in favour of temporary War Emergency Commissions for the duration of hostilities, and replaced the 18-month training courses at Sandhurst and Woolwich with Officer Cadet Training Units (OCTUs) intended to produce large numbers of officers more quickly.

The first batch of trainees under the new system were men holding university or school Officer Training Corps (OTC) qualifications or equivalent, after which all new officer trainees were selected from those serving in the ranks. This was less radical than it seemed, since conscription directed all available men into the armed forces anyway.

Selection for officer training was based on academic qualifications and interview. In practice, though some good NCOs were put forward, it still tended to be upper or upper middle-class recruits who were selected, partly because they were better educated and more likely to have some base of military knowledge from school cadet corps or university OTC.

However, these subjective methods failed to produce enough candidates, and a relatively large number (25–30 per cent) of those put forward failed the training. From 1942, the aptitude tests used to assign recruits were also used to identify potential officers, with around 6 per cent of recruits scoring as potentially suitable for officer training.

These attended three-day War Office Selection Boards (WOSB) that involved assessments, interviews and group command tasks instead of the previous short interviews. The selection boards proved much better predictors of which men would complete officer training successfully, and failure rates fell significantly.

The social background of Army officers broadened notably during the war, with middle-class grammar school boys largely replacing the public school-educated officers who had dominated the pre-war Army but made up only 25 per cent of the officers trained under the new system.

Cynics argued this was simply because there were no longer enough public schoolboys available and the boards often picked the grammar school boys who most closely resembled them in outlook. However, most agreed that the WOSB testing was far more meritocratic than the old process, and increased the supply of officer trainees while reducing failure rates to around 8 per cent.

The Army believed that its officers should be leaders first and technicians second, but officer trainees received a concentrated six-month training course covering driving, maintenance, gunnery and signals, followed by four weeks of tactics and crew handling before taking the WOSB tests.

Those who passed went on to the six-month OCTU course proper. Looking back, some officers felt that this was too 'academic', using sand-table exercises to teach tactics rather than time in the field with troops.

Robert Boscawen recalled that in 1942, 'We saw little of the tanks themselves and, for the most part, drove about in trucks. At other times we bicycled along the lanes in close groups of four, pretending to be tank crews sitting in the real thing!' (Boscawen 2001, p.4)

Valentine tanks of 6th Armoured Division being unloaded from railway flatcars for exercises in June 1941. Tanks were moved by rail wherever possible, to preserve their short engine and track lives, but loading and unloading from the narrow wagons was a difficult and sometimes hazardous procedure. The Valentine was one of the few early war British tanks that could be upgraded to carry a larger gun, although this meant the loss of both the coaxial machine gun and the loader in some versions, impairing combat efficiency (© IWM H 10984)

Each tank carried a tarpaulin, which could be rigged to the side of the vehicle as a bivouac. This example seems to be either camouflaged with paint or made from captured camouflage material. (Cody Images 1015 054)

CONDITIONS OF SERVICE

Life on camp

Accommodation during training and in camp was often spartan. Troops lived in draughty wood and corrugated iron Nissen huts, heated only by a solid-fuel stove, while ablutions blocks often only had cold water.

Soldiers slept in double-tier bunks, with bedside lockers for their kit. Each squad was responsible for its hut, and room chores had to be completed before PT and breakfast.

Reveille was normally at 0630hrs. Soldiers' working days could be dominated not by training, but by maintenance work on vehicles and the camp itself, and many UK-based troops resented apparently meaningless inspections and make-work during the long period of inaction between 1940 and 1943.

The Army realized that men worked better if they understood why they were doing things, and organized regular talks about the progress of the war and other current events to keep soldiers engaged.

A variety of sporting activities (especially football) were organized regularly for both recreation and physical training.

Men not doing extra duties as punishment could take advantage of on-camp amusements, such as the NAAFI canteen and usually a free cinema. Live entertainment (of variable quality) was provided by ENSA, or by amateurs from the unit itself, while the Army Education Corps put on a variety of classes, allowing men to continue their education.

Those who could get passes to nearby towns often looked for romance (or at least its substitute, sex) with local women at dances. Most thought sexual morality became looser during the war, though British soldiers often lost out to better dressed and better paid American GIs or more glamorous RAF aircrew.

Food

Food in barracks generally consisted of porridge, bacon with beans or tinned tomatoes and bread and butter for breakfast; fresh eggs were rarely available. Lunch was usually a sandwich or sausage roll, eaten in the field during

Crews lived off 'compo rations' when they could not be fed centrally from field kitchens. Several crews from 1st Northamptonshire Yeomanry divide up 14-man crates prior to Operation *Totalise*, August 1944. The appliqué reinforces on the sides of their Sherman provided extra protection to the ammunition bins. (© IWM B 8796)

training. The evening meal was often stew or 'meat and two veg' with gravy, followed by a stodgy dessert such as spotted dick with custard.

Although this menu might look uninspiring, it was adequate in calories and given wartime food rationing, it represented more food than most civilians enjoyed at the time. For recruits who had grown up during the depression, simply getting regular meals was an improvement, regardless of quality.

Officers ate the same as their men in the field, but ate in a separate officers' mess in barracks, with generally better cooked food and small luxuries such as wine, funded by subscriptions.

In combat, troops were fed from field kitchens where possible. These usually offered porridge for breakfast, and stew of some sort for the evening meal. Fresh bread was sometimes available from field bakeries, though infrequently enough to be worth comment in diaries. Overall, field kitchens provided about two-thirds of the Army's food during the North-West Europe campaign, but the proportion was much lower for the more mobile armoured units.

Troops lived on field rations when no field kitchen was available. Before 1942, these consisted mainly of Great War-style tinned corned beef ('bully') or bacon, hardtack biscuits and tinned margarine, processed cheese, jam or marmalade. These might be enlivened by occasional treats such as tinned peaches, but were not a balanced diet and quickly became monotonous – Pip Roberts noted 'we lived on "bully": fried for breakfast, cold for lunch and bully-stew for supper' (Roberts 1987, p.33).

From 1942, these were replaced by the composite ('compo') ration, which was essentially a wooden case of tinned food designed to feed a small unit for a day. Each compo pack contained one of seven main meals (menus A–G), plus instant oatmeal porridge, hardtack biscuits, tins of jam and cheese, chocolate, boiled sweets, matches, toilet paper and cigarettes. Tank crews received both five-man AFV packs, and standard 14-man packs, which were either split over two to three days or between several tanks.

Each AFV was issued a petrol cooker, though crews in the desert often improvised simple 'Benghazi Burners' by cutting a petrol 'flimsy' in half and filling it with petrol-soaked sand. Compo rations were also heated by piercing the cans and tucking them behind the tank's hot exhaust to warm through.

Food was invariably accompanied by copious amounts of tea. This was included in the rations either as powder or compressed into blocks, with sugar and powdered milk already added. If nothing else, the taste disguised the taint of chlorine, used for water purification. When available, tinned condensed milk turned a mug of tea into a small luxury.

Troops augmented their rations wherever possible. In the desert, this might mean pasta, olive oil and tinned tomatoes from captured Italian supply dumps or eggs and occasional sheep traded from the Bedouin. In France and the Low Countries, eggs, milk, cheese and vegetables were often given by the locals, or traded for ration chocolate and bully beef.

Alcohol rarely seemed in short supply. In addition to the infrequently issued (but usually appreciated) rum ration, Calvados could be traded from Norman farmers or (in one case) champagne liberated from Wehrmacht stocks. Being drunk remained a court martial offence, however.

Most men smoked, and round tins of cigarettes were included in each 'compo' ration, enough for a half-dozen each per day. Extras were snapped up, even dire wartime brands like Victory V. Aside from smoking them, cigarettes were useful currency when bartering with locals.

Pay

Pre-war regulars and wartime conscripts were paid on the same scale, although the actual amount depended on rank, length of service and allowances for special skills or trades.

Wartime British money had 12 pennies (d) to a shilling (s), and 20 shillings to a pound (£).

New recruits were paid 2s per day, or 14s per week. This was low given the average agricultural labourer was paid £2 10s per week, but the Army provided the soldier with food, accommodation and clothing.

By the end of their training, most tank crewmen had at least one trade – gunner, driver or radio operator – which attracted another 6d to 1s per day in proficiency or trade pay. Promotion and time served also increased pay – a junior corporal received at least 4s a day, while a tank commander would often be a sergeant, receiving at least 6s per day.

British troops often complained they were paid far less than their American equivalents – a US Private was paid the same as a British Lieutenant – and grumbled about low pay. However, some admitted they were better off as soldiers than as unemployed civilians during the 1930s depression.

Most men had part of their pay (typically half) sent to their families at home, and were paid the remainder at weekly pay parade. The men queued up before a table with an officer and a clerk sitting at it. Each soldier stepped forward in turn, saluted, and gave his name and service number. He then handed his pay book to the clerk who confirmed the amount due, and paid it in cash. The soldier saluted again, about turned and left.

Payment in the field followed the same pattern, but usually only happened when the unit was out of the line. The Army provided everything the soldier needed, and there was little to spend money on in the front lines anyway, so most men were content for their back pay to accumulate. Troops abroad were paid in local currency, or Allied occupation money.

Discipline and punishments

Some disciplinary problems are inevitable, especially as many soldiers were conscripts unused to military discipline. Most were dealt with at unit level, in accordance with the King's Regulations and the Manual of Military Law.

A crewman of a Sherman artillery OP tank chalks the name 'Al Capone' on the barrel of his vehicle's 75mm gun, April 1944. Vehicles were usually named, though bright paint was dulled down for camouflage after D-Day. Waterproofing for the D-Day beach landings has been applied to the gun mantlet and hull machine-gun opening. (© IWM H 37995)

Soldiers could be 'put on a fizzer' (charged with an offence) by any NCO or officer. For most offences – drunkenness, being absent without leave (AWOL), overstaying a pass away from camp, minor insubordination or performing a task badly – the case was heard and punishment ('Jankers') determined by the company or regimental commander.

Punishments might include being given extra fatigue tasks or especially unpleasant ones, being fined one or more days' pay or being reduced in rank ('losing a stripe'). Men could work their way back to their previous rank, and some went up and down the ranks several times.

Alternatively, the offender might be confined to the guardroom or put on 'change parade', having to report for inspection in various orders of dress (PT kit, best battledress, overalls etc.) in quick succession throughout the day and evening, an exhausting and frustrating experience unless the rest of his squad rallied around to help.

Serious offences (such as desertion or assaulting a superior officer) were dealt with by court martial, which could hand out stiffer sentences, including spells in military prison. Courts martial did not execute soldiers for cowardice or desertion, unlike the Great War.

There was less concern over the niceties of discipline at the front. Officers recognized men were under pressure, and using formal punishment could be counter-productive, since a man sent to the rear for court martial was safer than his comrades at the front.

CLOTHING AND UNIFORM

British soldiers, including tank crewmen, were issued two sets of battledress as their basic uniform. One set was usually kept as 'best battledress', with a full set of insignia, to be worn for guard duty, parades and formal occasions, while the other was kept as an everyday uniform.

Battledress consisted of short blouse-type jacket with shoulder epaulettes and two buttoned chest pockets, plus high-waisted trousers with a map pocket on the left thigh and a special field dressing pocket on the upper right thigh in addition to the usual hip and seat pockets.

PICKING UP A NEW TANK, WESTERN DESERT, EARLY 1942

Since all tanks came from outside the theatre, efficient tank recovery and repair of knocked-out tanks to get them back into action became extremely important for both sides in the desert.

The crew of a tank put out of action by mechanical troubles might take over a new vehicle together, but often the new crews collecting repaired tanks had been assembled from survivors of knocked-out tanks mixed with inexperienced new replacements. Some had the unpleasant experience of taking over hastily repaired vehicles that still bore evidence that their previous occupants had died aboard them.

Here, fitters dressed in two-piece denim overalls tension the tracks and clear the sand filters of a Crusader II tank before handing it over to its new crew. The fitters' tea is boiling on the inevitable 'Benghazi Burner' made from a cut-down petrol tin, though the NCO needs to keep his left hand over the top of his mug to keep flies out while he drinks it – a very common desert memory.

Tank transporters like the Scammell in the background were invaluable not only for recovering immobile tanks, but also for moving operational tanks around theatres without using up their relatively short track and engine life.

The vehicle next to it is another Crusader which has been fitted with a 'sunshade' of painted canvas over a metal strut frame, which makes the tank look like an innocuous truck to fool enemy air reconnaissance.

A Grenadier Guards corporal from the Guards Armoured Training Wing at Pirbright shows the 'textbook' uniform for an armoured crewman in 1943. He wears early concealed-button battledress, RAC steel helmet and blancoed 1937 web braces, with extenders to link them directly to the web belt rather than to ammunition pouches. The webbing was worn more to help extract wounded men from tanks than to support equipment; and carries only a long strap RAC holster. (© IWM TR 1410)

Jacket and trousers could be buttoned together, and were produced in a brownish wool serge fabric which provided some burn resistance. A simplified 'utility' version with exposed plastic buttons was introduced during the war to save fabric and production time.

Best battledress was worn as 'walking out dress' when on a pass and even on leave; clothing rationing meant soldiers might not have other clothes, and being in uniform avoided the social pressures against military-age men who weren't 'doing their bit' for the war effort. 'Best BD' was sometimes modified with an open collar, for wear with a tie.

Battledress was worn over a long, collarless pullover shirt, while trousers were held up by braces, like contemporary civilian trousers.

Crewmen were also issued a two-piece set of overalls. These were similar in design to the utility battledress, but produced in a greenish cotton denim fabric. They were intended for wear over battledress to protect it when doing dirty jobs, and were cut large. However, their cooler fabric meant they were sometimes worn instead of woollen battledress in hot climates.

There was a good deal of latitude in dress in the desert, as seen in these RTR soldiers posing atop a Matilda II wearing an assortment of battledress, overalls, sweaters and greatcoats. (© IWM E 7241)

The RTR issued similar 'coveralls' in black, so that oil stains would not show. These were rarely seen after 1941 except for maintenance duties, as their colour absorbed heat in the desert and stood out from background.

Tank crews were initially issued standard double-breasted, calf-length woollen greatcoats. Although warm and somewhat waterproof, these were impractically long for wear inside vehicles, and were sometimes cut down into hip-length 'shorties'.

Sleeveless leather jerkins lined with blanket material were also issued and worn, along with a variety of pullovers, including civilian school and cricket sweaters. Some men even wore pyjamas under their uniforms for extra warmth in very cold weather.

Crewmen wore standard black-leather army 'ammunition boots', though without the usual metal hobnails, since these skidded on tank decks and turrets. Some crewmen wore the issue rubber-soled plimsolls, which gave good grip on armour, or even occasionally carpet slippers. Crepe-soled suede 'desert boots' were common in the Middle East. Rubber wellington boots (supplied in units' chemical decontamination equipment) were sometimes worn in very wet weather.

Troops in the Middle East were issued shirt and trousers or shorts in a dark sand-coloured aertex cellular fabric known as Khaki Drill (KD), which were often bleached almost white by strong sunlight and repeated washing.

The pullover three-button shirt was often worn as an outer garment, and had a fixed collar, intended to be worn open. It had two flapped breast pockets and long sleeves, but troops often wore these rolled, or had them shortened to just above the elbow.

The shorts came in several patterns, but most were full cut and rather long, coming almost to the knees. Some units forbade vehicle crews to wear shorts, since long trousers gave more protection against burns.

Dress regulations in the desert can best be described as 'relaxed'. Troops often appeared to wear whatever they felt comfortable in. Cavalry officers in

A Sherman crew of 29th Armoured Brigade warm themselves around a petrol stove in a Belgian village, January 1945. The warm 'pixie' oversuits were invaluable in such conditions. The full-length zips allowing it to be put on or taken off without removing boots can be clearly seen on the leftmost soldier. (© IWM B 13424)

particular often wore a range of privately purchased clothes that bordered on the eccentric, as satirized in the wartime 'Two Types' cartoons. This might include civilian corduroy or moleskin slacks, coloured shirts and four-pocket 'Bush jackets'. Brightly coloured scarves were common, used as sweat rags and to protect the mouth and nose from sand and dust while driving.

Desert nights could be extremely cold, and troops could be seen wearing battledress blouses, greatcoats, wool balaclavas and (for officers) even sheepskin poshteen coats.

Limited numbers of special 'tank suits' were issued from 1942. The first pattern was a one-piece, button-fronted jumpsuit, made in heavyweight light brown cotton duck material, presumably to blend against both desert and temperate backgrounds. It featured wide epaulettes, hip and field dressing pockets plus a map pocket on the left thigh. A special revolver pocket on the right thigh replaced the holster, but the weapon hung awkwardly, and the pocket was dropped from future suits. Strong webbing tapes were sewn to the inside, running around the crotch and under the arms, ending in a prominent webbing 'handle' at the collar, to help extract an injured crewman.

This was replaced in 1944 by the 'Denim tank suit', which replaced the two-piece overalls and could be worn over battledress, or on its own in warm weather. It was another button-front, one-piece design, and was dark green when issued but faded with washing. It featured flapped pockets on both sides of the chest and both legs, plus hip, seat and field-dressing pockets. It lacked the revolver pocket and internal rescue harness of the 1942 suit, though the shoulder epaulettes were strengthened.

A cold-weather version was also developed, known as the Oversuit, Tank Crew or less formally as the 'pixie suit'. This was intended as a universal garment, worn over underwear in summer, and over battledress in winter, replacing the greatcoat. It was made of heavyweight waterproofed cotton, lined with woollen blanket material. It had a detachable hood and full-length zips down each leg, allowing it to be put on or removed easily while wearing boots or zipped together as a sleeping bag. It had two flapped pockets on the chest, two hip pockets, two map pockets on the front thighs, two large pockets on the lower legs, field-dressing pocket and three internal pockets. The pixie suit was originally manufactured in light tan material which made the wearer rather too visible, though most rapidly became stained with dirt and oil. A few were manufactured in camouflage material, at the very end of the war.

All tank suits had internal braces to support the suit when its pockets were loaded, and also allowed them to be worn with the top half rolled down. Insignia were not worn on them, though some officers and NCOs sewed on rank badges.

Many of the KD items used in the Middle East were also used in Burma, dyed dark green. Crews also wore the standard 1943 jungle green uniform – resembling battledress, but in cotton fabric – or just shorts and vest.

A special 'jungle tank suit' was produced in lightweight greenish-khaki cotton at the very end of the war. It resembled the denim tank suit, but with buttoned cuffs and drawstring ankles to keep insects out. It featured a rear seat flap which allowed the wearer to relieve himself without removing the suit, useful given the stomach upsets common in the tropics.

Goggles were essential for drivers and commanders, keeping dust raised by the tracks out of the eyes, whether in Normandy or the desert.

Whatever uniform was worn, it was usually filthy from mud, cordite and oil stains after even a short time in combat. Men rarely got to take off their clothes, let alone wash or change them, and the fabric absorbed the stench of cordite from the guns as well as sweat.

As one officer said in Normandy: 'These are tank crews. I don't care if their brasses are not polished as long as the breeches of their guns are clean and oiled, and their tank engines are running smoothly' (Tout 2007, p.166).

EQUIPMENT AND PERSONAL WEAPONS

Headgear and webbing equipment

Ammunition pouches were unnecessary for men without rifles, while water bottles and binocular cases were generally stowed inside the vehicle, rather than worn. Crews usually wore a reduced set of 1937 pattern webbing, with just a holster and pistol ammunition pouch. The web belt could have supported this alone, but shoulder braces were also supposed to be worn, since they could be used to lift injured crewmen through hatches.

The RAC issued a special open-top holster (Case, Pistol, Web, RAC) with a long strap suspending it from the belt to sit at mid-thigh level. In theory, such holsters were easier to draw from while seated, and would not catch on hatch openings while exiting the vehicle. In practice, the long strap snagged on projections inside the vehicle, and from 1942 the straps were shortened so the holster sat just below the belt. Crews also started to receive the full flap holster used by other troops.

Respirator haversacks were often worn in the 'alert' position on the chest during the 1940 campaign, when gas attacks were expected, but rarely after that. Indeed, crews rarely wore any webbing except the pistol holster and belt after 1940, as it was inconvenient aboard a tank and slowed any escape.

Crewmen of 1st Fife and Forfar Yeomanry in France, March 1940. They wear the later (1940) British 'Helmet, Crash, RAC' and respirators in the 'alert' position on the chest. This held the mask ready for use but was awkward for hatches. (© IWM F 3184)

The classic headgear associated with British tank crewmen is the black beret, worn by the Royal Tank Corps from 1924 and adopted by the rest of the Royal Armoured Corps in November 1941. This was practical to wear under headphones, and didn't show stains.

Men from cavalry and yeomanry regiments wore the rather impractical Field Service sidecap, or regimental equivalent, and sometimes continued to do so after they should have switched to the beret. Cavalry officers sometimes wore peaked Service Dress caps, though these were difficult to wear while using headphones or tank periscopes.

Several patterns of 'crash helmets' were adopted, to protect heads from the various protrusions inside tanks. The first version (Helmet, Crash, Royal Tank Corps) was issued in 1936 and had a two-piece compressed-fibre shell, while the second 1940 pattern was made up from six segments of canvas-covered cork.

A Sherman crew in the Western Desert, October 1942. Three wear American M1938 helmets, supplied with the vehicle but generally unpopular with British crews. Note the pullovers and braces (usually hidden beneath battledress) and hip field dressing pocket on the leftmost man, who has an intercom microphone round his neck. (© IWM E 18696)

Both had a thick padded 'bumper' at the front, to protect the forehead and face, and wide fabric cheek-pieces to hold earphones in place could be laced to the shell. Neither offered any ballistic protection, and were hot and generally unpopular, usually only being worn during training in the UK in the early years of the war.

Some American Lend-Lease tanks came complete with US M1938 crewman's helmets, which had a rigid resin-bonded shell pierced by ventilation holes and hinged earflaps to take headphones; it was little more popular than its UK equivalent.

Since the tank helmets offered no protection from bullets or shell splinters, crews were issued with standard British steel helmets. These worked adequately in open vehicles like carriers or scout cars, but were impractical in tanks, since the wide brim snagged on hatch edges and prevented using optical devices or headphones. The helmets were either stowed outside the vehicle for wear when dismounted, or simply discarded.

A special RAC steel helmet was issued from mid-1942, replacing all the earlier helmets. This used the shell of the airborne steel helmet, combined with the liner and chinstrap from the infantry helmet. It fitted the head much more closely, making it more practical for use inside vehicles. However, the shape resembled German 'coalscuttle' helmets, leading to occasional dangerous cases of mistaken identity in poor light.

Personal weapons

Although the tank's guns were their primary weapons, crews were also issued double-action Enfield .38 revolvers for personal defence. Crews received both the standard model and a special version with the hammer spur removed, to prevent the weapon accidentally cocking itself in the holster by catching on internal equipment.

Men of 4 RTR practising with their revolvers in a farmyard near Arras, October 1939. All wear black RTR overalls and the original long strap pistol holster. With gas attacks expected, they wear respirator haversacks, slung out of the way behind the hip. (© IWM O 493)

Each tank also carried a submachine gun (usually a US Thompson, especially on Lend-Lease tanks, but sometimes a British Sten) plus six hand grenades. This was intended for dismounted sentry duty or to guard prisoners, rather than as a bail-out weapon.

Many tanks also carried a Bren Light Machine Gun for anti-aircraft use as part of their equipment, along with 4 x 100rd AA drums. In practice, however, crews usually just closed up under air attack, rather than exposing themselves to fire back.

Crews sometimes acquired or scrounged other weapons. Captured German Luger pistols were popular souvenirs, along with various submachine guns for close-quarter defence in jungle or bocage.

INSIDE THE TANK

Crew positions

Tank crews varied from two to seven, depending on vehicle. Most tanks needed crews of four or five, with each crew position having its own responsibilities. Crews usually received some cross training, and might change job when promoted or moved between vehicles.

The driver was responsible for most maintenance on the vehicle, as well as driving it. Even the latter required making the best use of cover in action, rather than just getting from place to place.

Simply driving a tank was no easy task and small men sometimes found it physically hard to work the controls. Steering was usually via a pair of levers, one controlling each track, though the Churchill used a tiller bar. Slowing one track while keeping the other running pivoted the vehicle around the braked track, but turning too sharply could cause the vehicle to break or shed a track, which would take hours of backbreaking work to fix.

Equally, while tanks possessed better mobility than wheeled vehicles, they could still bog down in mud or soft sand. At the best, this meant hours of work to extract the vehicle. At worst, it could be fatal, leaving the tank an immobile sitting duck under fire.

The driver could rarely see the edges of the vehicle even with his seat raised to put his head and shoulders out of his open hatch. When the vehicle was closed down for action, his view was reduced to what could be seen through his narrow periscope, making him very dependent on the commander for guidance. Many tanks had a co-driver, who relieved the driver on long road marches, helped with maintenance and operated the hull machine gun.

Radio operation was a distinct skill with the fragile valve radios of the period. These needed constant cosseting, and could easily be knocked off the correct unit frequency by jolting cross-country travel or the main gun firing. Operators were also expected to send and receive Morse code as well as voice traffic, though this was rarely done in action.

The gunner aimed and fired the main armament and the co-axial machine gun mounted alongside it. The gun was aimed through a telescopic sight, with graduations built into it to help the gunner adjust for range. However, the sight had a narrow field of view, and the gunner was largely dependent on the commander to spot targets for him. Out of action, the gunner was responsible for maintaining the vehicles' weapons.

As main guns became larger, a separate loader was added to the crew, often doubling as the radio operator. Some early tanks expected the commander to double as loader, but it was difficult for him to do either job well and combat effectiveness suffered.

The loader's job was to select the ammunition type required (AP or HE) from the racks around the vehicle, and load it as quickly as possible; if the first round missed or failed to penetrate, a quick second shot could mean the difference between life and death. The loader usually worked standing, unlike the other crew members, as ammunition bins were spread around the vehicle. Most tanks had a folding seat for them when the vehicle was travelling. Out of action, he was responsible for re-stowing the tank's ammunition.

The tank commander was usually an NCO, though one tank in each troop was commanded by the troop's officer. His job was to pick out the best route for the driver, spot targets for the gunner and integrate his tank tactically into the overall troop plan. Commanders generally travelled with

CREW POSITIONS AND RESPONSIBILITIES

The Cromwell was the last major wartime development of the British Cruiser tank concept, first seeing action in Normandy. It was faster and had a lower silhouette than its US equivalent, the Sherman. However, Jake Wardrop, who served aboard Shermans before converting to Cromwells, was unhappy to do so, since he regarded the Cromwell as a much inferior vehicle and more cramped internally. It was significantly more reliable than earlier British designs, though still needing more attention than a Sherman.

Shown here are the crew positions in a Cromwell. The turret crew moved with the turret, which was divided by the breech of the gun. The gunner (**1**) usually had no hatch of his own, and had to follow the commander (**2**) out through his. The loader/radio operator is at (**3**) and the driver at (**4**).

While a five-man arrangement was typical, the Sherman Firefly replaced the co-driver's position (**5**) with extra ammunition stowage, to hold more of its large shells. Equally, the smaller Valentine tank had no co-driver/bow gunner, and had only two turret crew in some versions, which reduced the rate of fire and overloaded the commander, with consequent loss of fighting efficiency.

heads out of their hatches for better visibility. This made them vulnerable to shrapnel and snipers, but if the tank was forced to 'close up', the limited vision made them extremely vulnerable to enemy infantry tank hunters and concealed anti-tank guns. Indeed, snipers and machine guns often co-ordinated with Panzerfaust teams to target commanders and vision blocks to 'blind' a tank during an attack. Out of action, the commander had to navigate and map-read, and was responsible for the administration and discipline of his crew.

Crew communication

The noise inside tanks made normal speech almost impossible in action. Early tanks had rubber 'speaking tubes' for the commander to tell the driver which direction to turn, or even used string 'reins' attached to the driver's shoulders, but these were obviously inadequate.

By 1940, most tanks were equipped with WS19 radios, or equivalent. This combined two radios (the 'A set' for communication between squadrons and a shorter-ranged 'B set' for talking within each troop) with an intercom connecting headsets worn by each crew member.

A pair of buttons on the commander's microphone switched from intercom to radio net. Inevitably commanders sometimes forgot which button was pressed, and some scathing opinion or rebuke meant only for his own crew was broadcast to the entire unit.

Any set transmitting on a given troop or squadron net blocked any other set from transmitting on that net. Good radio procedure was essential to avoid jamming the net with irrelevant messages, though some yeomanry units took time to learn this.

Crewmen got much of their impression of what was going on from their wireless headphones. Many recall the calm voice of their officer over the radio as major steadying factor in action. Others heard men trapped in burning tanks screaming over the net as they burned to death.

Sergeant Yorke of 13th/18th Royal Hussars in the turret of his Sherman, May 1944, showing the radio/intercom headset and microphone. He wears a denim tank suit, with its distinctive pen loops on the breast pockets. It is unlikely that any commander would expose himself like this in combat. (© IWM H 38968)

Orders within a crew were given in a clear, concise format ('Gunner – target: tank, five o'clock, range 600') though this might be abbreviated as crews grew used to each other. Other signals were non-verbal, such as the loader slapping the gunner's leg as the breach closed, to let him know the gun was reloaded.

Conditions in a tank

Tanks were extremely cramped, filled with ammunition, rations and other necessities as well as the crew. Interiors were painted silver or gloss white to reduce the claustrophobic feel, but rarely stayed clean as crewmen came in through the hatches with muddy boots. Some men taped family photographs or pin-ups to the interior of the armour.

The breech of the main gun divided the turret interior in two, especially as it recoiled into the turret after firing. Turret crewmen usually sat in a rotating basket which turned with the turret; they could see the driving compartment through gaps in the basket, but moving from hull to turret was awkward.

The air inside tanks closed down for action could be almost unbreathable, especially in the stifling heat of Egypt or Burma. Aside from the unwashed bodies and uniforms of the crew and petrol fumes from the engine, acrid cordite fumes from firing the guns could build up until the crew had to open the hatches regardless of danger or be physically sick.

Closed-down crews urinated into spent shell cases that were passed up to the commander to be emptied out of a hatch, while solid waste went into machine-gun ammo boxes, which had an airtight seal.

Visibility was extremely limited when closed down, to what could be seen through small armoured glass vision blocks and periscopes. These gave most crew members a very restricted field of view, so they formed their impression of how the overall battle was going from the wireless chatter, as much as from what they could see directly.

The driver's compartment of a Valentine. The periscope is immediately in front of his face, showing the grip to turn it from side to side. When closed down in action, this provided the only view outside. He holds the intercom microphone, which also has a neck strap to hold it in place while driving. (© IWM E 9766A)

Commanders had controlled their vehicles with heads out of the hatch for better visibility in the open spaces of the desert, but such behaviour risked a sniper's bullet in tighter European terrain and a high percentage of commanders became casualties. This Churchill commander from 6th Guards Tank Brigade in August 1944 uses the armoured flaps of his hatch for protection. Extra armour has been added to the rear of the cupola, to protect the rear arc and avoid his head being silhouetted. The double triangle fitting on the right of the picture is the commander's sighting vane, which let the commander line the turret roughly onto a target, before handing over to the gunner with his telescopic sight. (© IWM B 9154)

Elaborate stowage diagrams showed where every item should be placed inside a tank, but in practice crews acquired a variety of additional possessions, useful items and loot. Vehicles often took on a 'gypsy caravan' appearance, with bedrolls, boxes of rations, deckchairs, and even cages of chickens lashed to the outside.

An obvious disadvantage was that such stowage was outside the armour, and many crews ruefully recall returning from action to find their stowage lockers riddled with shrapnel or small-arms fire, and ruined clothing and personal effects mixed with tinned fruit or stew from pierced tins.

UNIT STRUCTURE

British tank units went through several changes of organization during the war. Equally, local conditions or shortages of men and equipment meant units might differ significantly from 'official' establishment.

The RTR originally used infantry-style terminology of battalions, companies and platoons until it merged into the RAC in 1939, with each RTR battalion becoming a numbered regiment divided into cavalry-style squadrons and troops. RTR 'privates' became 'troopers' at the same time, though old-timers sometimes clung to the former term.

Each regiment had three fighting 'Sabre' Squadrons plus a HQ Squadron, and was commanded by a lieutenant-colonel, with a major as second-in-command. Each squadron was made up of three to five troops, and was commanded by a major, with a captain as second-in-command.

Each troop consisted of three to five tanks. One was commanded by the troop's officer, while the others were commanded by NCOs. Troops were usually commanded by lieutenants, although officer casualties sometimes meant they were led by the senior NCO.

Light Tank Mk VIs and lorries of the 8th Hussars assembled for an exercise in the Egyptian desert, June 1940. The fibre 'sun helmets' were hangovers from the inter-war period, and were rarely seen once hostilities started. Note how many softskin vehicles were needed to support even these machine-gun armed light tanks. (© IWM E 152)

Not every crewman in a tank regiment was aboard a tank. Each regiment included a troop of two-man scout cars for liaison and reconnaissance. This Dingo from 40 RTR wears Light Stone paint despite being in Sussex in December 1941, as the regiment was about to embark for the Middle East. (© IWM H 16292)

The three Sabre squadrons were not always equipped with the same tanks. One squadron was sometimes equipped with lighter tanks for a reconnaissance and pursuit role, while in the Desert Campaign, shortages meant some units fielded whatever vehicles were available.

The HQ Squadron typically had a two-tank HQ troop, a recce troop of light tanks, an intercommunication troop with armoured cars and an AA troop of anti-aircraft tanks. However, this varied through time, e.g. the AA troops were generally disbanded in late 1944 and their crews reassigned to regular tanks, in the absence of a significant air threat.

This fighting echelon was supported by an 'A Echelon' of unarmoured vehicles and trucks assigned to each squadron. These resupplied the fighting vehicles with fuel, ammunition and rations at temporary leaguers near the front lines.

It also provided specialist support, including the unit medical officer (mounted in an armoured half-track to evacuate wounded under fire), and the REME fitters Light Aid Detachment with a half-track and an armoured recovery vehicle.

The 'B Echelon' only came forward when the unit was out of the immediate front line and included baggage, a field kitchen and the officers' mess truck. Tank crewmen might be temporarily rotated to duty with the echelon as a way of resting them after heavy combat, though quite how restful it was to drive unarmoured trucks loaded with fuel and ammunition within artillery range of the enemy is debatable. Indeed, the fluid warfare in

A Scammell tank transporter carrying an A9 Cruiser tank to the workshops for overhaul, July 1941. Transporters were essential in the desert, for moving tanks the long distances to the front without wearing out their tracks and engines, and to recover damaged vehicles for repair. (© IWM E 4232)

the desert sometimes saw rear echelon vehicles attacked by enemy armour. The B Echelon also contained a number of spare tank crewmen, to provide casualty replacements and a nucleus to rebuild the unit around. Some crewmen welcomed being 'left out of battle' as a rest or an escape from danger, while others resented it or felt guilty about their mates going into action without them.

Personnel numbers varied according to the type of tanks the unit was equipped with. A Sherman regiment in 1944 had a nominal strength of 36 officers and 630 other ranks, manning 61 medium tanks and 11 light recce tanks, plus around 100 soft-skin support vehicles.

A TANK CREW'S DAY

Drag your weary body out of the turret, fill up with petrol and ammo, clean the guns, get something to eat, sleep, with only an average of three hours a night. How the hell did we manage to keep going? (Watt 2006, p.111)

Crew working on their Churchill tank in Italy, July 1944. This version is a 6-pdr armed Mk IV, though later versions had 75mms. Removing the centre track guard was common, as it could jam the turret rotation if it was damaged. The driver is adjusting the track tension; the vehicle could shed the track if this was mis-set, with serious consequences. (© IWM TR 2017)

ABOVE LEFT
Cleaning the bore of a 3 RTR Grant tank's sponson-mounted 75mm in the Western Desert, February 1942. The gunner and loader were responsible for cleaning the main gun and all machine guns, and reloading the vehicle with ammunition. Note the colour variation between battledress (left) and overalls. (© IWM E 8580)

ABOVE RIGHT
An 8th Armoured Brigade Sherman crew in a mixture of overalls and battledress, loading 75mm ammunition near Xanten, March 1945. The 75mm rounds had to be stripped out of their outer cases and inner packaging, and a full load of 75mm and machine-gun ammunition for a Sherman weighed around a ton. The vehicle has been fitted with extended end connectors ('duckbill grousers') to spread its weight and avoid sinking in the German winter mud. (Cody Images 1017962)

A tank crewman's day started early on operations. The entire unit usually 'stood to' just before dawn, with all weapons manned and ready against a dawn attack. It might then move out of its night leaguer position at first light, in case the location had been discovered overnight.

After the 'stand to', the crew prepared breakfast – usually tinned bacon or biscuits with jam or processed cheese – and the day's first mug of tea. They began the morning checks on their vehicle – checking oil levels and track tension, ensuring the radio was correctly tuned to transmit and receive on the troop and squadron nets etc. – while the vehicle commanders received a briefing from the troop or squadron commander.

The unit then moved out on the day's task. This might be a deliberate attack on a prepared enemy position, or an advance to contact, moving forward until the enemy was encountered.

Whatever the task, operating the tank and keeping a constant look out for concealed enemy positions was hard physical and mental work. Halts provided an opportunity to brew up tea, but food was usually limited to chocolate, boiled sweets and ration biscuits with cheese or jam, passed forward to the driver and commander and eaten on the move.

Tanks were vulnerable to enemy infantry during the hours of darkness, and needed daily resupply, so they pulled back to leaguer positions at night, to meet up with their supporting echelon. The tanks of the three Sabre squadrons formed three sides of a square, with HQ Squadron forming the fourth side and the unarmoured transport vehicles inside. Sometimes, either the tanks or the support vehicles had difficulty finding the leaguer, especially in the featureless desert, resulting in frayed tempers.

Work continued after the leaguer was reached. Each tank needed several hours of maintenance after a day of operations, including cleaning the main gun bore and stripping and cleaning all the machine guns.

The vehicle then had to be rearmed and refuelled. A full ammunition load for a Sherman included 97 x 75mm shells (9kg each) and 4,750 rounds of .30-calibre machine-gun ammunition, in 19 x 250rd boxes (10kg each). This totalled more than a ton of ammunition alone, and the crew had to pry open the wooden outer packing crates before loading it aboard.

ABOVE LEFT
A crewman refuels a Crusader from a 4-gallon 'flimsy', October 1942. Dozens of these were needed to fill a single tank, and after jolting across the desert in a truck, many would have split open along their seams and spilt their contents along the way, unlike the sturdier German Jerrycans. The crewman's boot soles lack the usual hobnails, which would skid on the armour. (© IWM E 18640)

ABOVE RIGHT
Breaking a track to repair a damaged or broken link was a back-breaking job for the whole crew. Note the infantry telephone box retrofitted to the rear of this 146 Regiment RAC Grant in Burma, April 1945. (© IWM SE 3747)

Refuelling was equally back-breaking – a full fuel load for a Sherman was 140 gallons (635 litres). This all had to be lifted above head height onto the rear engine deck in 32 x 25kg jerry cans before being poured into the fuel tanks.

Once their vehicles were ready for the following day's operations, crews could look after their own needs. The evening meal was usually stew from a field kitchen if they were lucky, or 'Compo' rations, washed down with more tea.

There was rarely time (and often not water) for a full wash; crews might be able to clean oil from their hands, but rarely more. Most slept in their dirty uniforms, removing the outer layer and boots at most.

Crewmen were issued a pair of woollen blankets and a groundsheet each. The usual practice was to lash one side of the vehicle's tarpaulin sheet to the side of the tank, while the other side was pegged to the ground to create a simple bivouac.

Sleeping inside the tank was possible, though uncomfortable, and crews might do so if there was a significant risk of mortar or artillery fire, rather than spend time and energy digging a slit trench.

Sleeping under the tank was not recommended, partly because of apocryphal stories of tanks on soft ground settling on sleeping crews and crushing them, and more practically because the oil sumps leaked. However, some crews did so if expecting mortar fire or heavy rain.

Crews rarely got a full night's sleep even once they did turn in. Men from the support echelon might provide leaguer sentries, but normal practice was for two men at a time from each vehicle to stand guard, rotating through the night. Sometimes, one vehicle in a good fire position was used as a 'guard tank'. Men from each crew then did two-hour stints manning that vehicle through the night, which meant the regular tank crew had outsiders clomping round 'their' tank all night.

Repeated days of this routine left crews exhausted from hard work and insufficient sleep. Unit Medical Officers could give out Benzedrine tablets to counteract fatigue, but these were only a temporary solution and had side effects if taken for prolonged periods.

Crews bedded down next to their Crusader tanks, Western Desert, August 1942. This is a posed photo, since no bivouac is rigged and nobody is up and moving despite it being full daylight. Note the stowage rack added to the front glacis. The Crusader was fast, but unreliable and even up-gunned versions only mounted 6-pdrs. (© IWM E 16262)

Time out of line

Soldiers did not fight continuously, even in combat theatres; both machines and men would have broken down within weeks. Instead, units were rotated out of line for rest and refit, while fresh units kept up the pressure on the enemy.

On other occasions, units were held out of line simply because the Allied supply chain could not provide all the advancing units with the food, fuel and ammunition they needed for offensive operations. Such lulls occurred in all theatres, but were particularly notable in late 1944, where bringing supplies forward across the damaged transportation net from the Normandy ports remained a bottleneck until the port of Antwerp was cleared.

A unit would typically be pulled out of line for a few days to a week, giving time to receive replacement tanks and crews, and allowing the men to catch up on sleep, eat decent meals and relax a little from the constant stress of combat.

If the unit were lucky, there might be a mobile bath unit, or at least the chance for them to wash uniforms that might not have been changed for weeks. If water was not available, clothes could be washed in petrol, which acted like dry-cleaning fluid. However, such laundry needed to air dry thoroughly afterwards, since any petrol residue caused skin irritation.

Units on rest in France and the Low Countries were often billeted in the homes of local people, who could be almost embarrassingly grateful. Many memoirs describe French or Dutch householders giving up their own beds so that liberating troops could have them, though Italian and German civilians were understandably less friendly. At

Sherman crews write letters home and catch up on their laundry while waiting to cross the River Seine, August 1944. (© IWM B 9775)

The Army provided what amenities it could for troops during rest periods at the front, including mobile cinemas, mobile bath units and mobile libraries, here being used by tank crews from 2nd Armoured Brigade, October 1942. (© IWM E 18028)

worst, the troops were accommodated in barns or schools, which were at least watertight and considerably better than tents, particularly in winter.

The first few days out of line were filled with hard work, as the men caught up on maintenance, resupply and chores to get themselves and their vehicles ready for immediate action again, if necessary.

After that, crews usually spent two to three hours on vehicle maintenance each day, and had the rest of the time to relax. Vehicle wireless sets were retuned to pick up the BBC, though this was officially frowned on as it drained the batteries. Depending on circumstances, there might be a mobile cinema or dances organized with local girls. Other diversions could be eccentric; 3 RTR organized tortoise races during one rest period in the desert. Alternatively, the men could just read magazines or paperbacks, and play cards or football.

D **BRITISH LEES IN EVENING LEAGUER, BURMA 1944**

After a day in action, the crews of these Lee tanks still had hours of work getting their vehicles ready for the following day's operations before they could rest. The close fighting in Burma led to tanks being fitted with add-on protection against Japanese limpet mines and demolition charges, and required very close co-operation with infantry, such as the Bombay Grenadier seen here in the steel helmet. Crews often stripped to the waist during the sweltering heat of the day, but regulations insisted on long trousers and shirts with unrolled sleeves after twilight, for protection from the ubiquitous malaria-carrying mosquitoes. The Lees arrived with their original American commanders' cupolas, but these were often removed, both to reduce the vehicles' high silhouette, and because they were too cramped for the commander to use the machine gun effectively.

Many wrote letters home. These were censored by troop commanders, who generally disliked the job, but were sometimes bewildered to find the most unprepossessing crewman might be conducting 'hot' penpal relationships with half a dozen different girls back home.

Crewmen often had girlfriends or wives and children in Britain, and letters from home were eagerly received, especially by troops in the desert or Far East. Not all brought welcome news, however; some crewmen, away from home for long periods, found themselves receiving 'Dear John' letters from girlfriends who'd taken up with new beaus, while Bill Bellamy learned in March 1945 that his mother had been killed in an air raid.

Officers caught up on administration, including fuel and ammunition returns, awards and promotions for experienced men, and reorganizing crews to spread experience when integrating replacements.

One unhappy duty for officers was writing the so-called 'deeply regret' letters to families of soldiers killed in action, to supplement the terse War Office telegram they would already have received. These had an almost standard form; men were invariably described as being well liked by their comrades, and as having been killed instantly without suffering ('never even knew what hit him') whatever the actual circumstances.

Aside from this time out of line, individuals or crews were granted short periods of leave. In the desert, this usually meant a few days in Cairo or Alexandria, or a rest camp on the coast.

In Europe, men became eligible for leave after six months. This might be a few days in Brussels or Antwerp, though the more fortunate received seven days in Britain (plus travel time). To ensure fairness, most units allocated leave slots by lottery.

Men also received ten days' embarkation leave before going abroad to the Middle or Far East and home leave (usually 21 days) when they returned. This was often all too short. Bill Close remembers: 'We landed at Glasgow on Christmas Eve 1943. I had been parted from my wife Josie for just over three years, and my son Richard was now a sturdy lad' (Close 2013, p.104).

MORALE AND CREW COHESION

Some men reacted to their call-up with trepidation, while others were actually eager to get into action before the war finished.

Despite the pacifist sentiments common in the 1930s, almost everyone felt the war was necessary, and that Britain and its allies would ultimately triumph. Even in the darkest days after Dunkirk in 1940, Ministry of Information surveys showed an overwhelming majority believed Britain should fight on, rather than sue for peace.

If anything, this determination increased as the war continued. Most soldiers knew people killed, injured or made homeless by German air raids, and were exposed to years of well-constructed government propaganda until few doubted the Axis countries had to be defeated.

However, these abstract beliefs did less to keep most men fighting than the presence of their comrades around them. Stuart Hills recalled: 'My greatest fear throughout the whole campaign had been to be thought a coward by the men I commanded. I can honestly say that I would have preferred to die than to let that happen' (Hills 2002, p.228).

A soldier of 50 RTR shaves besides his Valentine tank, with a photograph of his wife and new baby propped up alongside his shaving mirror, Western Desert, October 1942. Note how the paint has been scuffed and worn by the crew boarding the vehicle. (© IWM E 17880)

Unit loyalty was encouraged through the Army's traditional regimental system, though some trappings, such as dress uniforms, disappeared under wartime pressures.

RTR regiments did not recruit from particular areas, while even the Yeomanry regiments – theoretically linked to particular counties – often became thoroughly mixed as the war went on.

Ideally, men stayed with their regiment for their entire military career, and considerable effort was made to get wounded back to their original units after they recovered, rather than assigning them to a replacement pool as the US Army did.

In practice, some units which took heavy casualties were disbanded and their surviving personnel used to make up the losses of others. Men might change regiment when their unit provided a cadre for experienced men for a new unit, and received a draft of new recruits or men from other units in exchange. For example, the Sherwood Rangers Yeomanry returned from North Africa in December 1943, and the men given up for cadre were replaced by 100 men from the Lancashire Fusiliers, with no tank experience.

Regiments used their history and traditions to instil loyalty and pride. The RTR celebrated Cambrai Day (20 November), with officers and senior NCOs serving rum-laced tea to the troops in bed, and observed this even in the field when possible.

The resulting bonds could be very strong. Keith Douglas, assigned to a safe staff job in Cairo, applied to rejoin his unit numerous times. He finally

The Cruiser Mk I (A9) mounted a 2-pdr gun and three Vickers machine guns, including two in archaic sub-turrets. It was fast, but suffered from being poorly armoured and extremely unreliable mechanically. It saw service in France, the early Desert Campaign and Greece. (© IWM KID 261)

'borrowed' a vehicle and set off – in direct disobedience to orders – across several hundred miles of desert to return to his unit during the Alamein fighting.

Tank crews bonded strongly under the pressure of living and working together in a confined space amid shared danger. They often knew each other better than anyone except their families, and still remembered their wartime crewmates decades later.

However, while the morale effect of keeping crews together was well understood, it was not always possible in practice. For example, 8 RTR lost 120 men in only three weeks of fighting in the Gothic Line, roughly 50 per cent of its tank crews. Such casualties would affect almost every crew in the regiment. Even if their own tank was not disabled, men had to be taken from existing crews to provide some leavening of experience to replacement crews or promoted to fill gaps left by casualties.

Men were often part of several crews during their time in action, if they avoided becoming casualties themselves. At the most extreme, Ken Tout recalls taking over a tank whose commander had been injured and going into action without even knowing the names of his crew.

Such fighting inevitably took a toll; even the most unimaginative crewman knew horrific injuries could be waiting around the next corner. Particularly dangerous jobs like acting as lead tank were rotated between tanks in a troop, for fairness. Even so, most men were under severe psychological strain, and some failed under it.

After D-Day, British tank crews quickly found their vehicles were outclassed by the newer German designs. As Jake Wardrop commented after examining a knocked-out Panther, 'I took a good look at it and decided that I would examine no more of them, as it was bad for my morale' (Forty 2009, p.143).

Even the Sherman Firefly, which had firepower equal to a Tiger, had nothing like the same level of armoured protection. Rightly or wrongly, it became commonly accepted that it cost three to four Shermans to kill a Tiger. This obviously had serious morale effects, and every German tank easily became 'a Tiger' to scared crewmen.

Many noticed that units with considerable battle experience from the desert were much more cautious during the European campaign than newly raised units, and that all crews became much more reluctant to take chances after the fighting reached Germany and the end of the war was in sight.

On the other hand, liberating French and Dutch towns was a massive boost to morale. Aside from the obvious appeal of being met by cheering crowds and pretty girls happy to kiss any Allied soldier, it provided clear proof that the Germans were being driven back.

During the Desert Campaign, most British tank crews appear to have regarded their German adversaries with respect rather than animosity, and seen the Italians as somewhat hapless. Attitudes hardened as the war continued; some crews had regarded machine-gunning escaping German tank crew as 'unsporting' in 1941, but did so without hesitation in 1945.

Most British troops in Burma seem to have hated the Japanese from the start, and few expressed any thoughts of compassion or mercy towards them.

Since the Japanese rarely showed either of those qualities themselves, such attitudes were understandable.

Some units regarded relatively formal relationships between ranks as a key part of military discipline. In others, experienced enlisted men could address NCOs and the commander of their own tank by first names, even if he was an officer.

A combination of better-educated enlisted men and a broadening of the social background of the officer corps narrowed the gap between officers and men compared to the Great War. It narrowed further during the war, as officers lost some of their privileges, though some gap remained until the end.

Not everyone felt this was a good thing; some pre-war regular officers felt that many wartime junior officers were jumped-up NCOs without the experience of the traditional 'officer class' in handling men.

Each regiment had a padre to offer spiritual support. Sunday church parades were compulsory in camp, but there are few atheists in slit trenches, and the optional services in the field were usually well attended. 'Most of the congregation would not have been regular church-goers in civilian life, but they relished praying in such adverse circumstances and were undoubtedly sincere as they did so' (Hills 2002, p.143).

BRITISH TANK DESIGN

At the start of the war, British doctrine distinguished three classes of tank, each with separate roles.

Light tanks were fast, and lightly armed and armoured. They were intended for 'imperial policing' against irregular opponents on the North-West Frontier or in the Middle East, and for scouting. Both functions were largely taken over by armoured cars as the war developed.

Infantry tanks were dedicated infantry support vehicles. They were relatively slow, since they were tied to the pace of the infantry they supported, but relatively well armoured.

Cruiser tanks were intended for independent action, filling a 'cavalry' role. They were relatively fast, to outflank and cut off enemy units, but at the price of having lighter armour.

In practice, any tank had to deal with whatever tactical situation and opponent it found itself facing, and they ultimately merged into general purpose 'universal' or 'medium' tanks.

British tank designs suffered from poor mechanical reliability during the early years of the war. This was most notable in tanks like the A13 Mk III Covenanter, which was so unreliable the 1,800 built never saw action, and were only used for training in Britain.

Even the Churchill, which became a mainstay of the British tank force, was initially issued with a caveat in its handbook admitting that early models had 'a few features ... which may give rise to troubles not normally expected in service'. These would normally have been solved before adoption, but the rush to get it into service meant they had to be fixed afterwards instead.

The American-built Stuart was only a light tank, but had almost the firepower of a British Cruiser, and delighted crews with its reliability. This example from the Western Desert in 1942 is laden with stores and personal kit. Note the helmet used to protect the headlamp. (© IWM E 16455)

Britain received some standard US-made M3 Lees with the US turret (right) and a version fitted with a new British-designed turret known as the Grant (left). Lees and Grants served in the Far East and the desert; these are with the 4th (Queen's Own) Hussars at El Alamein, July 1942. The M3's sponson-mounted 75mm gun was invaluable, even if the vehicle itself was a stopgap until the Sherman – mounting the same gun in a turret – reached production. (© IWM E 14053)

The situation eventually improved, although British designs invariably needed considerably more maintenance to keep them running than their US equivalents until the end of the war.

From 1941, Britain began to receive significant numbers of US light and medium tanks under the Lend-Lease programme. Aside from the simple numbers of vehicles received – the M4 Sherman became the most common tank in the British inventory – the US tanks were notably reliable and had good general-purpose 75mm guns.

The balance of advantage in tank design swung back and forth during the Desert Campaign as both sides upgraded their tanks and introduced new ones, and for a while crews of the US-supplied Grant and Sherman tanks had the welcome experience of out-gunning their opponents.

By D-Day, however, technical superiority had swung back to the Germans. While the Panzer IV – still the most common German tank – was roughly

A Valentine DD tank, January 1944. These were used extensively for DD crew training, though only Sherman DD tanks were used operationally. The crew wear life-jackets, and those in the hull wore Davis submarine escape sets, to give them some chance to get out if the vehicle sank. British DD tanks did much better than their American equivalents on D-Day, as British landing craft crews realized the sea was rougher than expected and launched them closer to shore than planned, while many of the US DDs – launched at the planned distance – were swamped and sank. (Armor Plate Press)

The Firefly was based on the US-built Sherman, but up-gunned to take the very powerful British 17-pdr, which was capable of killing any German tank. However, only limited numbers were available. The massive flash and recoil, plus the difficulty of handling the long, heavy ammunition in the cramped turret slowed a second shot, making first-round accuracy vital. (© IWM B 5546)

equivalent to a British medium, the newer Panther and Tiger tanks were significantly better armed and protected. They were able to destroy British tanks well beyond the effective range of the British tank's own guns, and required good use of terrain and co-ordinated tactics to outflank and defeat.

In fact, the British and (especially) US emphasis on tanks that could be produced in large numbers, rather than being individually powerful, was probably correct from a strategic viewpoint. Post-war analysis indicated that although the Tiger might be a better tank than the Sherman, it consumed several times the resources to build, and rarely achieved enough kills to justify the additional resources. However, such considerations were little comfort to men in the front line.

Tank armament and gunnery

> Snowie orders 'Gunner, fire! Reload HE. Driver, swing left. Co-driver, fire when on.' I stamp on the firing button of the 75mm, then on the co-ax button. The huge breach of the 75mm leaps back into the turret, jams against its springs, slides forward again into place. It thunderclaps in my left ear. The automatically opened breach coughs stifling cordite fumes. In my telescope the mighty muzzle flash of the 75mm obscures and blinds momentarily as a tracer spark leaps across the brief space and slams into the ground by the German machine gun. Our tank rocks back on its haunches under the power of the 75 recoil. Streaks of smaller tracer from our co-axial Browning follow the same trajectory as the larger shot, sparking around a hardly visible dug-out … All this within a second, without breathing, without thought. Our 75 had been loaded with AP, not necessarily effective against men in a hole in the ground but a very discouraging package to receive … Tommy is ramming a high-explosive shell into the breech. He slaps my leg, signing 'loaded'. (Tout 2007, p.59)

An A34 Comet advances through a ruined German town. The Comet was the last British Cruiser design to actually see combat during the war. It was a good design – essentially an improved, up-gunned and up-armoured Cromwell – but only became available in limited numbers from December 1944. (Armor Plate Press)

A tank's weapons were central to its purpose; the whole point of the vehicle was to move and protect gun, crew and ammunition.

Although some early war light and infantry tanks were armed purely with machine guns, most mounted a main gun, plus machine guns for close defence.

The main gun normally fired several types of ammunition. Armour Piercing (AP) ammunition was designed to penetrate the armour of other tanks. However, as most AP rounds were essentially solid projectiles, they had little effect on other targets, though they were useful against very solidly constructed bunkers.

High-Explosive (HE) rounds would generally not penetrate tank armour, but their burst effect was very useful against infantry, soft vehicles such as trucks or anti-tank guns. Once HE rounds became available for tank guns, they quickly dominated ammunition loads, which were typically 75 per cent HE.

Smoke rounds were used to conceal the tank, or to mark targets for other weapons. Some smoke rounds were phosphorous-based, and could set buildings on fire.

Despite pre-war expectations, the most common targets for tank guns were not other tanks, but anti-tank guns and infantry positions.

Early war British tanks were armed with the 2-pdr (40mm) anti-tank gun. This was a problematic choice, for several reasons. First, it was a high-velocity weapon optimized for firing AP, and its small calibre meant it could

Mounds of empty 75mm ammunition crates and packing tubes around this Sherman in the Anzio beachhead in May 1944 shows how much ammunition could be expended when firing indirectly. (© IWM NA 14606)

E TANK ACTION IN NORMANDY, 1944

The primary mission for British armour, such as these Shermans (**1**), was to help get the infantry forward, by eliminating machine-gun nests that would otherwise inflict very heavy casualties on them. Although Tigers and Panthers could inflict heavy losses when they appeared, Allied air superiority prevented many from even reaching the battlefield. Most British tank casualties were inflicted by well-concealed anti-tank guns or tank destroyers (**2**), which tactically resembled mobile armoured anti-tank guns more than they did tanks. Anti-tank mines (**3**) were used to channel armour into killing zones and inflict casualties, and machine guns (**4**) worked to make tanks close up and to suppress accompanying infantry, allowing tank hunter teams (**5**) to move in with Panzerfausts.

The British had developed the Sherman Firefly (**6**), mounting a very powerful 17-pdr gun capable of destroying any German tank. However, it lacked a good HE round, lost the co-driver and hull machine gun to accommodate the larger 17-pdr ammunition and suffered from a much lower rate of fire and turret traverse, making it vulnerable in close country. One was assigned to each four-tank troop, so that it could provide anti tank support for the regular Shermans, while they protected it from other battlefield threats.

Previous experiences in the desert meant the British put insufficient emphasis on working with infantry prior to Normandy. Lessons were learned, such as adding an external telephone at the rear of the tank (**7**) to allow infantry to talk to the tank crew without exposing themselves.

On the left, we can see casualties being evacuated by one of the regiment's two medical half-tracks (**8**), but bailed-out crews usually had to make it at least part of the way back on their own, since the half-tracks were obviously less well protected than the tanks themselves.

not fire HE or smoke rounds. A proportion of vehicles were therefore completed as Close Support (CS) versions armed with 3in. or 3.7in. howitzers, which could fire HE or smoke but lacked a decent AP round. It also meant that the majority of vehicles, armed with 2-pdrs, could only engage anti-tank guns with their machine guns, making them very vulnerable. Secondly, the 2-pdr was an adequate anti-tank weapon at the start of the war, but quickly became obsolete as the Germans fielded better-armoured tanks. Such developments were inevitable, but the British kept the 2-pdr as their main gun until 1941–42, by which time it was almost completely ineffective.

It was replaced by the 6-pdr (57mm), again based on an infantry anti-tank gun and optimised for AP, with the same issues about lack of a decent HE or smoke round.

US Lend-Lease medium tanks began to arrive in 1941, armed with a medium-velocity 75mm gun; the M3 Grant carried this in a limited traverse hull mount, while the M4 Sherman carried the same gun in a rotating turret. This finally gave British tanks a gun combining a decent HE round for use against anti-tank guns and infantry with decent armour-piercing performance against the German tanks of the time.

Later versions of Churchill and Cromwell tanks were armed with a British equivalent, firing the same ammunition. While the 75mm remained a good general-purpose weapon even after D-day, it struggled to penetrate the armour of the later German medium tanks such as the Panther, let alone the Tiger.

However, the British managed to squeeze their high-velocity 17-pdr (76mm) anti-tank gun into a Sherman turret, creating the Sherman Firefly. This was able to destroy any German tank, including the Tiger. Its lethality was further improved by the special Armour Piercing Discarding Sabot (APDS) ammunition which appeared at the very end of the war in Europe, though these were scarce and each vehicle often had only a half-dozen available.

Since the 17-pdr lacked a good HE round and relatively few Fireflies were available, only one of the four vehicles in a Sherman troop would be a Firefly, with the others being normal 75mm vehicles.

Crews were taught to fire on the move in the early years of the war, and pre-war regulars had often spent a good deal of time practising this. However, it proved too inaccurate in combat, and the 1941 manual accepted that firing from stationary was more accurate and effective. Of course, any tank halting to fire immediately became a sitting target for return fire. A well-trained crew that could halt, fire and be moving again quickly stood a much better chance of survival, as Bob Crisp describes:

> I completely discounted the possibility of shooting accurately from a moving tank, which was what we had all been taught to do when it was not possible to take up a hull-down position. So I worked out a system ... The first order, then, was 'Driver advance; flat out.' The gunner would do his best to keep the cross-wires of his telescopic sight on the target all the time we were moving. The next order, heard by gunner, driver and loader would be 'Driver halt.' As soon as the tank stopped and he was on target, the gunner would fire without further command from me. The sound of the shot was the signal for the driver to let in his clutch and be off again. From stop to start it took about four seconds. (Crisp 2005, p.21)

The 2-pdr was often mounted 'free', elevated by a stock resting on the gunner's shoulder, but this was unviable for heavier guns. Sherman gunners controlled their weapons with the hydraulic traverse in one hand and the elevation wheel in the other, with main gun and co-axial MG being fired by a pair of foot pedals.

Shermans enjoyed a higher rate of fire than their German opponents, since their shorter, lighter shells could be slammed into the breech faster, and their lighter turrets traversed more quickly. While this didn't fully make up for the less powerful gun, crews quickly learned that they had to shoot first and keep shooting when they encountered a Tiger or Panther, to disable it with sheer weight of fire or at least smash sights and tracks.

75mm-armed vehicles could be used for indirect fire. However, while it was tempting for crews to sit back and shell a target from a distance, this was often discouraged by unit commanders. It was less effective than regular artillery, used huge amounts of ammunition – Ken Tout remembers a shoot of 200rd per tank – and could lose the momentum of the advance.

Most tanks had a co-axial machine gun mounted alongside the main armament, which elevated and traversed with it. It was fired by the gunner, using the main armament sight, which had range graduations for aiming the MG as well as different main gun rounds.

Some early Cruiser designs had subsidiary one-man machine-gun turrets, in addition to the main turret. However, these were cramped, often proved death-traps for the occupant when the vehicle was hit, and were not effective enough to justify the extra weight.

Later tanks generally had a single hull machine gun instead, fitted in a limited-traverse mount and fired by the co-driver. 'Co-ax' and hull machine guns were used primarily to suppress enemy infantry, but their effective range was only around 500m from a moving tank.

Tanks ideally worked in pairs. Each vehicle covered the other since the limited visibility from within meant the covering tank could see infantry working around the sides of a tank or into its vulnerable blind spots better than that tank's own crew. However, jungle tracks or the narrow lanes of Normandy often forced vehicles into single file, preventing this protective overwatch. Crews learned to shell or machine gun any cover that might conceal enemy infantry as they moved forward, rather than waiting to be fired upon.

Finally, most tanks had smoke dischargers mounted on the turret, allowing the tank to create a smokescreen for concealment while it closed with an anti-tank gun, or cover its retreat if it ran into something it couldn't handle.

IN COMBAT

Casualties

A solid shell tore through the armour plating just above my head and buried itself in the wireless set at the top of the turret. Then several more penetrated and set the tank on fire ... These tanks burned high-grade aero petrol and in a matter of seconds the inside of the tank was a mass of roaring flames. The operator was out of the turret in a flash; he, too, had seen what happened when the ammunition exploded in one of these tanks. It was not an easy climb from the gunner's seat, but I was out of that turret faster than a champagne cork leaving the neck of a bottle. I had less than a second to spare, for as my feet touched the ground the tank exploded, and I saw the turret sail over my head … The Germans had obviously seen us bale out, and poured machine-gun bullets at us. I dropped down and crawled back through the sand. (Leakey and Forty 1999, p.97)

Despite the armour on their vehicles, some tank crewmen inevitably became casualties.

Sometimes, the vehicles themselves caused casualties. Fingers got broken or lost nails when trapped in closing hatches, while the commander's hatch on the Crusader and Covenanter was notorious for its weak catch. This let it swing forward if the vehicle stopped abruptly, smashing into the back of the commander's head, simultaneously concussing him and knocking his front teeth out against the front hatch rim.

More than a third of armoured unit casualties were outside their vehicles at the time: echelon personnel, casualties when leaguers were mortared, men who stepped on landmines or crews machine-gunned while escaping from their vehicles.

While few men equalled Bill Close, who had 11 tanks knocked out under him and survived, most crewmen had to bail out of at least one tank during their service.

The grim statistics showed that on average, each tank knocked out meant one crewman dead and another badly wounded. Commanders could become casualties even if their tank was not knocked out, as they routinely exposed their heads for a better view, even in action.

Troop commanders were also expected to immediately take over one of their subordinates' tanks if their own was disabled, to continue leading their troop, effectively doubling their risk.

When he joined as a replacement troop commander in Normandy, David Render was told his life expectancy was only two weeks, and indeed he was almost the only troop commander in his unit to get through the campaign uninjured.

Tanks were largely immune to small-arms fire and artillery fragments. High-explosive rounds were unlikely to destroy tanks, though they might break tracks and destroy external fittings, sights or antenna, and being trapped inside a tank under sustained artillery bombardment was a thoroughly unpleasant experience.

Anti-tank mines were commonly used on their own or as part of larger defensive schemes. They might injure crewmen – usually drivers – but commonly just broke tracks and roadwheels, immobilizing the vehicle. However, they were often sited to immobilize vehicles in the killing zone of anti-tank guns, or mixed with anti-personnel mines to kill crewmen who dismounted to fix the damage.

Demonstrating casualty extraction from a Matilda II turret using hoist and slings, August 1941. The Army experimented with several such systems, but none were remotely practical under fire, or in the short interval before a stricken tank's fuel and ammunition began to burn. (© IWM H 12542)

Tank crewmen killed in action were usually buried near where they fell, though if a vehicle burned, recovering and identifying the remains could be a literally nightmarish task. Reverend Victor Leach, regimental Padre of 13th/18th Royal Hussars, conducts a burial service in June 1944. (© IWM B 5184)

The main threat was armour-piercing (AP) rounds. These were solid projectiles, intended to punch through armour by simple kinetic energy. Although enemy tanks had been expected to be the primary threat, the majority of British tanks destroyed were actually victims of anti-tank guns. Mounted on low, wheeled carriages, these were sited to cover obvious approach routes and carefully camouflaged, making them difficult to spot before they opened fire. Since they invariably waited for a good shot before firing, they were almost guaranteed a first round hit, before the remaining tanks could react.

Rounds which failed to penetrate could 'spall' fragments off the inside of the armour, injuring crewmen. If the round did penetrate, things were far worse. The white-hot projectile ricocheted around inside the hull, striking crewmembers, fuel or ammunition. If either of the last were hit, there was a good chance of the tank catching fire. The likelihood of this depended partly on the tank. 'When the Churchill was hit it caught fire three times out of five, and it could take up to ten seconds for the fire to sweep through from the engine compartment to the turret. The American Sherman caught fire every time, and the flames swept through in about three seconds' (Wilson 1974, p.55). The Sherman was notorious for burning easily; Germans called them 'Tommy Cookers' and even their own crews sometimes referred to Shermans as 'Ronsons', after the cigarette lighter.

Fire was the crewman's greatest fear. Tanks were full of inflammable material – lubricating oil, fuel and especially ammunition – and about 25 per cent of crew casualties were from burns. Unsurprisingly, gunners – who lacked an escape hatch of their own, and had to follow the commander through his – were usually the most severely burned.

Getting out of the vehicle quickly was key to survival, but many tank hatches were little wider than a man's shoulders and drivers' hatches could be completely blocked by the gun in some turret positions. Equipment or headset cables could snag on projections. Worse, a powerful impact could distort the hull, jamming the hatches in their warped frames with the crew pounding at the inside.

If injured crewmen couldn't escape unaided, getting them out of a burning vehicle through a narrow hatch was nightmarish even if other crew members were unhurt and able to help. Various methods such as getting a rope under a casualty's armpits to lift him clear were taught during training, but official records frankly admit that all proved impractical under fire, and enemy tanks or infantry routinely machine-gunned escaping crews.

Crews received basic first aid training, and each tank carried two first aid boxes (one inside, one outside) containing dressings and morphine. Crews in the desert often prepared 'bail-out bags' containing water, maps and rations to sustain them until they were picked up.

A crew with injured men would try to get them back to the Regimental Aid Post as quickly as possible. This was usually the unit Medical Officer's armoured half-track, where he would stabilize casualties before sending them onward. Badly wounded men would go to a field hospital in theatre, which could involve several days' travel for men injured in Burma or the desert.

Casualties could accumulate very quickly in heavy combat, as Bill Close describes: 'so ended Operation *Goodwood* for 3RTR. It had been a hard battle with two days of heavy fighting. The battalion had lost well over sixty tanks with heavy personnel losses. In my own squadron I had lost seventeen tanks out of my complement of nineteen, over half being completely destroyed. All my officers were casualties, except Johnny Langdon, and only one troop sergeant, Buck Kite, was with me at the end. Practically every man in the squadron had bailed out at least once' (Close 2013, p.130).

Similarly, the 11 weeks of fighting in Normandy cost the Sherwood Rangers Yeomanry 200 casualties, including 50 tank commanders, around a third of its total strength and the majority of its tank crews, commanders and officers.

Dead crewmen were sewn into army blankets and buried abroad, though they might be moved from their initial hasty graves into formal military cemeteries after the war. Even identifying the dead from a burned-out tank was a horrific task. One unit's padre describes refusing help from tank crews to deal with such an incident: 'Buried the three dead and tried to reach remaining dead in tanks still too hot and burning … Fearful job picking up bits and pieces and re-assembling for identification and putting in blankets

BAIL OUT! ITALY, NOVEMBER 1944

The Churchill proved very useful in the mountains of Italy, its long track run and climbing ability allowing it to reach places no other tank could. However, the terrain favoured the defence, and this Churchill has been hit by a concealed anti-tank gun.

The first shot broke a track, immobilizing the vehicle. As this made the vehicle a sitting duck for subsequent shots, the commander ordered the driver and hull gunner to bail out while he tried to spot the flash of the gun and destroy it before it could also knock out the following tank. However, the gun hit the Churchill again before it could be located. The shot penetrated the turret, killing the gunner and injuring the commander.

The crew are very fortunate that the Churchill is not only relatively slow to burn, but had an escape hatch in each hull side, allowing the crew to escape without exposing themselves to the fire sweeping the top of the turret – machine-gunning crews escaping from stricken tanks was common practice by both sides.

The driver has recovered the tank's external first aid box – there was another inside, but crews did not always have time to grab it as they escaped – to administer morphine to the injured commander. However, they are in a perilous position – the gun may well put more shells into the tank to ensure a kill, quite possibly detonating the ammunition on board, but making a dash for it under fire and carrying a wounded man is extremely risky.

for burial. Squadron Leader offered to lend me some men to help. Refused. Less men who live and fight in tanks have to do with this side of things the better' (Hills 2002, p.90).

Not all injuries were physical. Troops distinguished men suffering from cowardice (which was looked down on) from those whose nerves were in tatters after prolonged fighting. It was acknowledged that even the bravest men eventually broke down under the stress of combat.

Rotating men out of the line to get decent food and sleep for a few days was generally successful in limiting the effects of this, but even so there were self-inflicted wounds and men breaking down under the strain. Around 10 per cent of casualties evacuated were psychological, though others stayed with their unit but were redeployed to tasks in the support echelons.

The fall of France (September 1939–June 1940)

Britain and France declared war in September 1939 over the invasion of Poland, but could provide little practical help before the Germans overran it.

Instead, much of the regular army – reinforced by mobilized reservists and territorials – was dispatched to France as a new British Expeditionary Force (BEF). British armoured forces were relatively numerous, but had few other virtues – of the tanks available, over 1,000 were thinly armoured light tanks mounting only machine guns. Only 164 were infantry or cruiser tanks, and even these were armed with 2-pdrs at best.

However, many German tanks were little better, and the French had a large force of modern tanks, mostly well armed and armoured if inefficient in their crew arrangements. Overall, the BEF was not a badly equipped force – its transport was entirely mechanized, for example, whereas the Germans still relied on horse-drawn vehicles and artillery. It was not material inadequacies which led to Allied defeat, but superior German tactics and training.

Light Tank Mk VIs of the Fife and Forfar Yeomanry, France, March 1940. At this early stage, only a few men wearing long strap holsters and RAC crash helmets rather than infantry tin hats mark these men out as tank crew. (© IWM F 3168)

The Allies unwisely stood on the defensive over the winter of 1939/40 (the so-called 'Phoney War'), allowing the worn-out German forces to recover from the Polish campaign and absorb its lessons. The Allies also spread their tank forces along the entire frontier, whereas the Germans concentrated theirs, gaining local superiority despite lesser overall numbers.

When the Germans attacked in May 1940, the Allies were fooled by a German feint and advanced into the Low Countries, anxious to meet the expected thrust as far forward as possible. Meanwhile, the main German forces pushed through the forested Ardennes, encircling the Allied spearheads and driving a wedge between the British and French armies.

With their supply lines cut, under frequent air attack and with enemies behind them, the BEF began to fall back on the Channel ports, away from the main French forces. The situation was made worse by lack of radios, so once a unit became scattered, it was difficult to reassemble.

Mechanical reliability was not a strong point of early war British tanks. Many suffered breakdowns or simply ran out of fuel during the long marches along refugee-choked roads. Lacking time or spare parts to repair them, many were destroyed by their own crews without meeting the enemy.

The British mounted a successful counterattack at Arras, which emphasized that although the Matilda II (of which the BEF had very few) was effectively proof against the standard German 37mm anti-tank gun, it could be engaged successfully by 88mm anti-aircraft guns and artillery.

Although the Arras counterattack was limited in scope, it contributed to the Germans halting their advance for several days to regroup. This bought time for 338,000 Allied troops to be evacuated from Dunkirk, far more than originally expected.

Meanwhile, further British forces, including 3 RTR, had been landed at Calais to help defend it and divert pressure from Dunkirk. However, their hurried dispatch meant vehicles were shipped separately from their ammunition, fuel, tools and crews.

Dockside confusion reigned as crews tried to organize themselves and their vehicles, which were sent into action piecemeal as they were ready. Ultimately, they managed only to briefly delay the fall of Calais before destroying their surviving vehicles and evacuating what men they could.

Overall, the British Army lost every one of the 700-odd tanks it took to France, and around half of their crews. Those who did make it back were initially used as infantry for coastal defence, as no replacement vehicles were available.

Cruiser Mk IV (A13) tanks of 5 RTR drive through a Surrey village, July 1940. The driver's visor is open for visibility; he would obviously close down in action. (© IWM H 2491)

Matilda tanks of 44 RTR near Worthing, December 1940. The Matilda was well armoured for its day, and popular with its crews. It served well in the early war campaigns, but could not be upgraded in the way German tanks were. The crew wear black RTR overalls, leather jerkins and wellington boots from the unit's gas decontamination supplies. (© IWM H 6371)

ABOVE LEFT
The crew of a Light Tank Mk VIB cook their Christmas dinner beside their vehicle in the desert, December 1940. Much of the early campaign took place in the Middle Eastern winter, when desert temperatures could be brutally cold. (© IWM E 1501)

ABOVE RIGHT
Flies were ever-present in some areas of the desert, and these casually dressed Crusader crewmen wear mosquito nets over their heads as they write letters home in August 1942. A dressing covers the equally ubiquitous 'desert sore' on the leg of the nearer man. (© IWM E 16270)

The Desert Campaign – early days (September 1940–February 1941)

Britain's strategic concern with the Suez Canal meant her only significant overseas armoured force was based in Egypt. The Italian dictator Mussolini had been massing forces in neighbouring Libya, and in September 1940 they invaded Egypt and established a number of large fortified camps.

The British counterattacked, despite being heavily outnumbered. Attacks on the camps were spearheaded by British infantry tanks, which were almost immune to any Italian weapon, and broke their resistance.

The British pursued the retreating Italians back into Libya and captured Tobruk. Meanwhile, the 7th Armoured Division made an outflanking move through the desert to block the Italian line of retreat, forcing most of their army to surrender after it failed to break through the encirclement.

The British had won a major victory, capturing 138,000 prisoners. However, their tanks were largely worn out from sustained operations. Combined with the need to send troops to protect Greece – despite the objections of local commanders – this prevented effective follow-up to drive the Italians from North Africa completely.

The Greek Campaign (March–April 1941)

The Greek Army defeated an initial Italian invasion in October 1940. However, concerned that Germany would reinforce her Italian allies, the British diverted forces from the Middle East to assist the Greeks, including two armoured regiments.

The British forces were dispatched to northern Greece, but encountered problems even before the fighting began. 3 RTR had left its new A13s in the Middle East and taken older A10s to Greece, but almost all the spare parts they received were for A13s they no longer had.

Greek resistance collapsed quickly once the Germans invaded, and the British tanks found themselves acting as rearguard during the retreat down the length of Greece, along icy mountain tracks.

The worn-out tanks suffered more losses from breakdowns than enemy action, not helped by the lack of spares and workshop facilities, which meant otherwise repairable tanks were destroyed by their crews.

Bob Crisp recalls: 'Of the 60-odd tanks 3R.T.R. had taken to Greece at the beginning of the year, not half a dozen were casualties of direct enemy action. All the others had been abandoned with broken tracks or other mechanical breakdowns' (Crisp 2005, p.15).

Some tank crews were evacuated before Greece fell, while others made their own escapes by ramshackle boats to Crete, before being sent back to Egypt. Once more, however, every vehicle was lost.

Although the Greek Campaign was disastrous for the British, it was ultimately even more disastrous for the Germans. Although they easily won the six-week campaign, it delayed the start of Operation *Barbarossa* and potentially prevented the capture of Moscow before the Russian winter.

North Africa – the Germans arrive (March 1941–May 1943)

British forces had decisively defeated the Italians, but were weakened by transfers to Greece. Hitler assisted his ally again by dispatching the Afrika Korps in March 1941. The British were pushed back again, but reinforced the Middle East to avoid another defeat.

Since the Mediterranean was dominated by Axis aircraft operating from Italy and Greece, troops reached the Middle East by a six-week sea voyage that swung far out into the Atlantic to avoid U-boats, then rounded the southern tip of Africa and ran up along the East African coast. How comfortable the voyage was depended on the ship, but most were crowded. They usually docked at Durban or Cape Town en route, with troops enjoying a few days' leave in a friendly city without blackouts or rationing.

More than any other battlefield, the desert – almost devoid of towns to defend and without rivers to block movement, so there was always an open flank to turn – resembled that envisaged by British inter-war advocates of 'Cruiser Tank' warfare.

It was a harsh place to fight. Bill Close recalls: 'Temperatures at midday were in excess of 110 degrees and life in the tank was almost unbearable; even the flies dropped dead inside. It was also possible to fry an egg on the back of the tank' (Close 2013, p.77).

Bully beef became semi-liquescent in its tins. Water was in short supply, and often brackish. Men saved water by scrubbing cooking utensils with sand rather than washing them, while even shaving was sometimes forbidden. Any movement churned up dust and grit, which irritated men's eyes, clogged mouths and nostrils and crunched between the teeth when they ate.

Heat haze made fighting during the middle of the day almost impossible. Khamsin sandstorms could last for hours or days, cutting visibility to a few yards and making any activity almost impossible. On the other hand, desert nights were bitterly cold, so crews bundled up in every piece of clothing they possessed. When rain came, it was torrential, causing flash floods and bogging down operations.

Flies were everywhere; men remember having to eat with one hand while waving off flies with the other, and still eating several of them with each meal. Minor cuts and grazes easily became infected 'desert sores' that didn't heal.

A Crusader tank with a canvas 'sun shield' camouflage frame and the middle three roadwheels blacked out with paint to make it look like a lorry from the air, March 1942. The large, open desert theatre meant these could be used to fool enemy air reconnaissance about the number and location of British tanks. (© IWM E 9876)

Navigation was difficult in the featureless terrain, and magnetic compasses were unreliable aboard tanks, because of the steel hull. One could compensate for this, but such compensations were thrown off by moving tools or ammunition within the vehicle. Even distance travelled was uncertain, as track slippage in loose sand made odometer readings unreliable. Units appointed specialist navigating officers, who used Bagnold sun compasses.

While British tanks outmatched their Italian equivalents, the technical balance tilted against the British when the Afrika Korps arrived. The German PzKpfw III and IV tanks were better armed and armoured than their British equivalents, and were repeatedly upgraded to maintain this superiority.

Until the balance shifted back, when 75mm-armed Grant and Sherman tanks arrived from the US, the German tanks could penetrate British tanks at much longer range than the British could penetrate them, forcing British crews to evade desperately while trying to get close enough for their own weapons to be effective.

Tactically, the headlong 'all guns blazing' charges that had put the Italians to flight proved extremely costly against the Germans, who lured British tanks onto screens of dug-in anti-tank guns – including the fearsome 88mm – then used their own tanks to deliver a counter-attack from the flank once the guns had mauled and disorganized the British.

The Desert War was dominated by logistics, with both sides supplied from ports at opposite ends of the theatre via long, tenuous supply routes. Any retreating force thus had the advantage of falling back on its own supply lines, while the pursuer's supply lines stretched ever longer. Afrika Korps operations were sometimes more constrained by the supply situation than by British forces, and suffered from having lower priority than the more critical Eastern Front.

The major British offensive in June 1941 (Operation *Battleaxe*) was a costly failure, with half the attacking tanks lost on the first day. The more successful (if equally costly) Operation *Crusader* (November–December 1941) relieved Tobruk and secured Egypt.

The Afrika Corps counterattacked in May 1942, capturing Tobruk and pushing the British back in disorder until their advance was stopped at El Alamein (July) and Alam el Halfa (August). The British – now under General Montgomery – rebuilt their forces before returning to the offensive with the second battle of El Alamein in October, inflicting a decisive defeat on the Germans.

A Sherman of 4th County of London Yeomanry fording the Volturno River, October 1943, fitted with wading trunks which were also used for beach landings. The Sherman was probably the most important tank in British service during the war, combining a gun capable of firing a decent HE round with excellent mechanical reliability. However, it was outclassed by newer German vehicles by late 1944. (© IWM NA 7859)

The US landing in Tunisia (Operation *Torch*) meant that the remaining Axis troops were caught between Allied forces on either side. Although the British advance into Tunisia – cooler and greener than the desert, with villages and olive groves – saw hard fighting until May 1943, Axis resistance only delayed their inevitable defeat.

The Italian Campaign (September 1943–May 1945)

With North Africa secured, the Allies agreed using the Eighth Army's experienced veterans to invade Italy and push into the 'soft underbelly' of Axis-held Europe would be easier than assaulting Hitler's Atlantic Wall in France, and might knock one Axis power out of the war completely.

In fact, Italy's long mountainous spine, with numerous rivers flowing down to the sea to both east and west, created a series of natural defensive lines. The Germans methodically defended each of these in turn, then fell back to the next, turning the campaign into a grinding series of assaults on fixed positions.

The collapse of the Italian government did little to help, as the Germans simply took over the Italian positions and continued their fighting retreat until Germany itself surrendered. Even the weather seemed hostile, with rain and cold all winter, then mosquitoes and malaria in the summer.

From Normandy to VE Day (June 1944–May 1945)
Although individuals and some units returned to the UK to help with training, most experienced British tank units were still fighting in Italy. The tank formations committed to D-Day thus lacked previous battle experience, unlike the German units they would be fighting.

Troops received a last leave to see families before D-Day, but once the pre-invasion briefings had been delivered, all troops were confined to camp for security reasons. Vehicles going ashore on D-Day and in the follow-up waves had to be prepared for deep wading to land directly on the beaches, by fitting extended exhausts and painstakingly sealing every aperture and the turret ring with mastic. The waterproofing was fitted over strings of cordite, to be blown off when the tank reached firm ground.

The initial landings went well, partly due to the immediate fire support from amphibious Sherman DD tanks coming ashore with the first waves, and other specialized armour neutralizing beach defences and obstacles. However, the breakout from the beachhead was slowed by the Normandy Bocage, with its dense hedgerows and sunken lanes. The plan required British forces to engage the Germans head-on and draw in the German armoured reserves, while US forces swung around and cut the Germans off. Although ultimately successful, this meant that British tank units endured repeated costly assaults against prepared positions defended by armour and anti-tank guns.

A Cromwell recovery vehicle crew is welcomed by Dutch civilians in Eindhoven, September 1944. Units often received joyful receptions from towns they liberated, boosting morale. The crewman has shortened the long strap of his open top holster to sit directly on the belt. (© IWM BU 950)

The close country also required tank–infantry co-ordination. As Stuart Hills put it: 'We needed the infantry to protect us from anti-tank weapons, and they needed our support to deal with the machine guns and small-arms fire which threatened their advance and killed so many of them' (Hills 2002, p.101). However, their experiences in the more open desert meant the British had neglected this, with tank and infantry units often paired up in an ad hoc manner rather than having trained with each other, and operating on different radio nets. Things improved with experience, but at a steep price in blood.

The bocage favoured the new German Panzerfaust disposable anti-tank weapons, which were short-ranged but could be carried by a single infantryman.

Cromwell tanks white-washed for camouflage, January 1945. The Cromwell was the closest British equivalent of a medium tank, and was faster and lower than the Sherman. However, it required more maintenance, and the flat armour panels didn't deflect projectiles as well as the Sherman's curves. A canvas muzzle cover protects the main gun bore. (Cody Images 132558)

These had not been available during the Desert Campaign, and might not have been particularly effective on the open terrain there. However, they became a major threat to tanks in Europe.

Memories of Normandy often mention collateral damage from the heavy fighting – destroyed farmsteads and villages, omnipresent dust and the stench of fields filled with bloated corpses of cattle killed by artillery bombardment rotting in the sun.

Once the breakout finally succeeded, British forces advanced rapidly across France, as the Germans hastily retreated to avoid the American encirclement. Units received joyous receptions as they drove through French and Belgian towns liberated without the heavy fighting and devastation which befell Normandy.

Some were disquieted by the aftermath of liberation, as the resistance took revenge by summarily executing supposed collaborators or humiliating women who had dallied with German soldiers by shaving their heads; others felt such things were understandable revenge for years of oppression.

This rapid advance – 'the great swan' – overstretched Allied supply lines, and some units found themselves forced to halt as they were temporarily stripped of their soft-skin echelon transport vehicles to keep the leading units moving. Unfortunately, this allowed the Germans to reorganize and stabilize the front.

 TANK CREWMAN IN NORTH-WEST EUROPE, WINTER 1944/45

British tank crews continued to wear battledress until the end of the war, but by the winter of 1944, most had been issued with the 'pixie suit' coverall, which could be worn instead of battledress, or over it.

The Besa (British tanks, **1**) or Browning (US Lend-Lease tanks, **2**) machine guns could be dismounted for ground use or cleaning. Crews often acquired Sten submachine guns (**3**) for close defence.

Intercom headsets (**4**) and the WS19 radio set (**5**) provided communications both within and between tanks, while the Verey pistol (**6**) provided a back-up and a means of communicating with units on different radio nets.

Personal items included the First Field Dressing (**7**) which all troops carried, and the AB64 Pay Book (**8**), which provided a record of service and qualifications as well as pay. It included a simple will form at the back, which men were required to complete. Crews were also issued the 'Guide for Troops in France' (**9**) to help them deal with the local population, and instruction handbooks for their vehicles (**10**). The Davis Submarine Escape Apparatus (**11**) was issued to crews of Sherman DD tanks, to allow them some chance to get out of their vehicle underwater.

Earlier rations had been replaced by 'Compo' (**12**), either in the standard 14-man box or the five-man AFV pack.

Ammunition for late-war British tanks was primarily either 75mm (**13**, AP and HE) or the very powerful 17-pdr (**14**, AP only). Machine-gun ammunition belts came in metal boxes, whether 7.92mm for Besas (**15**) or .30 for Brownings (**16**).

A crewman with a Sten guards two captured members of a bicycle-mounted anti-tank unit, April 1945. The short-range disposable Panzerfaust anti-tank weapons strapped to the handlebars of these bicycles could knock out a tank from ambush, and nobody wanted to be the last casualty of the war. The crewman has acquired a German MP-44 assault rifle as a souvenir. (© IWM BU 3197)

Meanwhile, the ambitious attempt to seize key Rhine bridges (Operation *Market-Garden*) failed – the bridges were captured by airborne forces, but the limited road net and stiffening German resistance prevented ground forces relieving them quickly enough. Deliberate demolition of flood defences meant that Allied units were more or less roadbound, creating logistic bottlenecks.

The fierce winter of 1944 effectively brought operations to a halt. Bill Bellamy recalls: 'It was too cold to see without goggles and yet impossible to wear them, as they froze on to your nose. If you took them off, in order to have a clear view, your eyes filled with tears, which either froze to your face or failing that, your eyelids froze shut' (Bellamy 2005, pp.173–74).

Tanks were painted with whitewash as temporary snow camouflage, but icy, frozen roads gave almost no grip to steel tank tracks even when they were not blocked by snow.

Many units were temporarily billeted in Dutch and Belgian homes, glad to be out of the weather, when the Germans counterattacked in December 1944. Much of this attack fell on US forces, and British armoured units defended key points while available supplies were diverted to the Americans.

Some units found themselves giving up their tanks and learning to operate Buffalo amphibious vehicles for the Rhine crossings in March 1945, the last major Allied operation in Europe before Germany finally surrendered in May.

The Far East (December 1941–August 1945)

The Japanese conquests of Malaya and Singapore had been shocking setbacks to the unprepared British. When the Japanese offensive continued into Burma, they seemed unstoppable, and forced another British retreat.

Burma was difficult tank country, but the limited number of tanks available – mostly light US-built Stuarts – proved invaluable during this retreat. They acted as rearguard, and provided vital armoured spearheads to break through numerous roadblocks – usually well covered by fire – established across the British line of retreat by Japanese troops infiltrating through the jungle. Tanks even carried wounded or exhausted infantry, saving them from certain capture when they were unable to keep up.

Sadly, these tanks were destroyed by their crews when the British force retreated back across the Chindwin River into India, as they could not be transported across.

Only a half squadron of Valentines was available to support the unsuccessful First Arakan Offensive (December 1942–May 1943), but some officers drew the incorrect conclusion that Burma was not suitable tank country, rather than that more tanks were needed.

The utility of tanks in Burma was conclusively proved the following year, during the Second Arakan Offensive. A single regiment of Lees was critical to the defence of the Admin Box, which had been surrounded by the Japanese and was being supplied by air. Their heavy firepower was vital for repulsing attacks, and they conducted small counterattacks almost daily, pushing back the continual encroachments the Japanese made on the edges of the box under cover of darkness.

Holding the Admin Box was the first defeat for the Japanese, and the turning point of the campaign. The attacking Japanese force essentially destroyed itself attempting to capture it, and failed to draw Allied reserves away from the Imphal and Kohima battles.

These saw the decisive defeat of Japanese attempts to invade India, and British and Indian Army tanks again played an important part. After that point, the British held the initiative and methodically pushed the Japanese out of Burma, ending with conventional armoured operations around Meiktila and Mandalay in March 1945.

Units had already begun training with amphibious DD Shermans for a seaborne assault on Japanese-held Malaya (Operation *Zipper*) when atomic strikes on Japan ended the war.

Throughout the war, tanks were vital to deal with Japanese bunkers. These were usually so solidly constructed as to be immune to small arms and artillery, and the only way to deal with them was often for a tank to painfully work its way close to the bunker, protected by infantry, then either blast it apart with repeated fire, or (if very close) post a round directly into the firing slot. Gunners had to aim such shots by opening the breech and looking down the bore, as the normal sights were displaced too far from the barrel axis to be used at such short range.

Tanks also provided extremely close support to infantry attacks, firing HE and MG over the heads of advancing infantry to suppress the defenders, then switching to AP (which had no blast effect) as the final assault went in. Tanks also carried extra ammunition and water for the infantry, and extracted their casualties.

Japanese tanks were rarely encountered, and were both outclassed by British vehicles and usually poorly handled by their crews. Equally, the Japanese had few anti-tank guns, and those encountered were a relatively low threat.

If the Japanese lacked sophisticated anti-tank weapons, they did not lack courage or ingenuity. Night infiltration attacks against leaguers were common, to kill crews outside their vehicles. Tanks were attacked with lunge mines – a hollow charge on a pole, detonated by ramming it against a tank, despite invariably fatal consequences for the user – or with grenades and limpet mines; many tanks were fitted with wire mesh to prevent the latter being fixed to the vulnerable top of the hull.

One Lee was even boarded by a sword-wielding Japanese officer, who killed the commander and 37mm gunner before being killed inside the turret by the loader. As they became more desperate, Japanese concealed themselves in pits with bombs or artillery shells, detonating them when a tank drove over their pit.

Because of such incidents, crews often defended themselves with Tommy guns, and an Indian Army unit – the Bombay Grenadiers – became specialists in providing close protection for tanks. Some units evolved standard procedures for mutual defence, so tanks being boarded 'closed up' and the Japanese were machine-gunned off the hull by a neighbouring vehicle.

Burma's mountainous terrain and tidal creeks meant that tanks often had to work their way into position along narrow tracks and up steep rocky or muddy slopes to where they were needed.

Tropical diseases such as dysentery and skin rashes were ubiquitous in the heat and humidity. It was almost impossible to conduct operations during the monsoon season, and long supply lines and lower priority compared to other theatres hampered logistics. Malaria-carrying mosquitoes meant that troops had to wear long sleeves and trousers after nightfall, and take anti-malarial Mepacrine tablets daily. Some tried to avoid these, as they turned the skin yellow and were rumoured to cause sterility, so officers watched men take their tablets.

RETURN TO CIVILIAN LIFE

Although conscripts were enlisted 'for the duration' rather than for a fixed number of years, labour shortages in the UK meant the government wanted to get men back into 'civvy street' as quickly as possible. Planning for this started well before the end of the war; lectures on the demobilization scheme began in September 1944.

Men were released according to age and time served, though those with skills important for post-war rebuilding could be released early. Men with the least time served would form occupation units in Germany, or transfer to the Far East for the continuing war against Japan.

Officers with 'wartime only' emergency commissions could apply to exchange their commissions for regular ones and remain in the Army, though the limited places available meant only those who passed a selection process were accepted.

The first men were released in June 1945, six weeks after VE Day and nearly two months before the end of the war, though the last troops from the Far East were not released until 18 months later.

Soldiers received a demobilization grant when they left the Army, along with a set of civilian clothing. This included a three-piece 'demob suit' plus shirts, underclothes, raincoat, hat and shoes. The clothes were made from good-quality fabric, although fit could be somewhat approximate.

They returned to a badly battered country, with serious housing shortages from the Blitz and food rationing until the early 1950s. Divorce rates spiked to levels not seen again until the 1960s, when returned soldiers found their wives had been unfaithful or wives found their husbands changed by years of war. On the other hand, there was full employment, and most readjusted rapidly.

World War 2 veterans remained part of the Army reserves for six years after demobilization, and some were recalled for the Korean War (1950–53).

MUSEUMS AND RE-ENACTMENT

The Imperial War Museum (www.iwm.org.uk) holds large archives of photographs, diaries and some vehicles at its London and Duxford (Cambridgeshire) sites. The Tank Museum (www.tankmuseum.org.uk) at Bovington (Dorset) holds an extensive collection of World War II British tanks, some of which can be seen running during the summer. The National Army Museum in London (www.nam.ac.uk) and the D-Day Museum in Portsmouth (www.ddaymuseum.co.uk) also offer useful collections.

BIBLIOGRAPHY AND FURTHER READING

Beale, Peter, *Tank Tracks: 9th Battalion Royal Tank Regiment at War, 1940–45*, Sutton Publishing, Stroud, 1995

——, *Death by Design: British Tank Development in the Second World War*, Sutton Publishing, Stroud, 1998

Bellamy, Bill, *Troop Leader: A Tank Commander's Story*, Sutton Publishing, Stroud, 2005

Boscawen, Robert, *Armoured Guardsmen: A War Diary, June 1944–April 1945*, Leo Cooper, Barnsley, 2001

Close, Bill, *Tank Commander: From the Fall of France to the Defeat of Germany*, Pen & Sword, Barnsley, 2013 (originally published in 2002)

Crisp, Major Robert, *Brazen Chariots*, W.M. Norton, New York, 2005 (originally published in 1960)

Delaforce, Patrick, *Taming the Panzers: Monty's Tank Battalions – 3rd RTR at War*, Amberley Publishing, Stroud, 2010

Douglas, Keith, *Alamein to Zem Zem*, Faber & Faber, London, 2008 (originally published in 1946)

Dyson, Stephen W., *Tank Twins: East End Brothers-in-Arms, 1943–45*, Leo Cooper Ltd., Barnsley, 1994

Fletcher, David, *The Great Tank Scandal: British Armour in the Second World War (1)*, HMSO, London, 1989

——, *The Universal Tank: British Armour in the Second World War (2)*, HMSO, London, 1993

Foley, John, *Mailed Fist*, Granada Publishing, St Albans, 1975 (originally published in 1957)

Forty, George, *Jake Wardrop's Diary: A Tank Regiment Sergeant's Story*, Amberley Publishing, Stroud, 2009

——, *Royal Tank Regiment: A Pictorial History*, Guild Publishing, Tunbridge Wells, 1989

Greenwood, Sergeant Trevor, *D-Day to Victory: The Diaries of a British Tank Commander*, Simon & Schuster, London, 2012

Grounds, Tom, *Some Letters from Burma: The Story of the 25th Dragoons at War*, Parapress Ltd., Tunbridge Wells, 1994

Halstead, Michael, *Shots in the Sand: A Diary of the Desert War, 1941–1942*, Gooday Publishers, East Wittering, 1990

Hamilton, Stuart, *Armoured Odyssey: 8 RTR in the Western Desert, 1941–42, Palestine, Syria, Egypt 1943–44, Italy 1944–45*, Tom Donovan, London, 1995

Hills, Stuart, *By Tank into Normandy*, Cassell Military, London, 2002

Holland, James, *An Englishman at War: The Wartime Diaries of Stanley Cristopherson DSO MC TD, 1939–45*, Bantam Press, London, 2014

Kershaw, Robert, *Tank Men: The Human Story of Tanks at War*, Hodder & Stoughton, London, 2008

Leakey, Rea and Forty, George, *Leakey's Luck: A Tank Commander with Nine Lives*, Sutton Publishing, Stroud, 1999

Leyin, John, *Tell Them of Us: The Forgotten Army – Burma*, Lejins Publishing, Stanford-le-Hope, 2000

Perrett, Bryan, *Tank Tracks to Rangoon: The Story of British Armour in Burma*, Pen & Sword, Barnsley, 2014 (originally published in 1978)

Plant, John, *Infantry Tank Warfare*, New Generation Publishing, London, 2014

——, *Cruiser Tank Warfare*, New Generation Publishing, London, 2014

Render, David and Tootal, Stuart, *Tank Action: An Armoured Troop Commander's War, 1944–45*, Weidenfeld & Nicolson, London, 2016

Roberts, Major General G.P.B., *From the Desert to the Baltic*, William Kimber, London, 1987

Taylor, Dick, *The Men Inside the Metal: The British AFV Crewman in WW2, Vols 1 and 2*, Mushroom Model Publications, Petersfield, 2014

Tout, Ken, *By Tank: D to VE Days*, Robert Hale Ltd., London, 2007

Urban, Mark, *The Tank War: The Men, the Machines and the Long Road to Victory*, Little Brown, London, 2013

Watt, Robert 'Jock', *A Tankie's Travels: World War II Experiences of a Former Member of the Royal Tank Regiment*, Woodfield Publishing, Bognor Regis, 2006

Wilson, Andrew, *Flame Thrower*, George Mann Ltd., Maidstone, 1974 (originally published in 1956)

INDEX

ammunition **A17–18** (11), 33, 33, 44–46, **44**, **G13–16** (59)
aptitude tests 8, **8**, 9, 13
armament and gunnery
    2-pdr guns 40, 44–46, 47
    6-pdr (57mm) guns 46
    17-pdr (76mm) guns **E6** (45), 46
    75mm guns 17, 33, 42, 43, 46, 47
    anti-aircraft guns **A10** (11), 25
    machine guns 40, **E4** (45), 47, **G1–2** (59)
    maintenance 33
    operation 26
    overview 25, 43–47

badges and insignia **A1–2** (11), **A19** (11)
bailing out 49–50, **F** (51)
Bellamy, Bill 38, 60
Boscawen, Robert 14
Bovington 8–9, 10

camouflage 15, 17, 55, 58, 60
camp life 15
casualties 47–52, **49**
Close, Bill 12, 38, 48, 50, 55
clothing and uniforms
    battledress **A** (11), 18–20, **20**, 33
    for DD tanks 42
    greatcoats 20, **20**
    hot climate wear 21–22, **D** (37), 54
    overalls 20, 25, 33, 53
    overview 18–23
    pre-war service dress 7
    pullover shirts 21, 24
    tank suits 21, 22, 28, **G** (59)
communications 28, **28**, **E7** (45), **G4–6** (59)
crew positions and responsibilities 25–28, **C** (27)
Crisp, Bob 46, 55

daily life 32–38
Desert Campaigns (1940–41, 1941–43)
    action 54, 55–56
    crew **B** (19), 20, 24, 35, 39, 54
    tanks **B** (19), 30, 32, 33, 35, 41, 42, 54
discipline and punishments 17–18
Douglas, Keith 39–40
drivers and driving 25–26, **C4** (27)
'duckbill grousers' 33
Dunkirk evacuation (1940) 53

the enemy, attitudes to 40–41

Far East Campaigns (1941–45) 34, **D** (36), 60–62
fitters **B** (19)
Foley, John 10
food and rations **A13–14** (11), 15–17, **16**, 33, 34, 54, 55, **G12** (59)
footwear 21, 34, 53
France, fall of (1940) 23, 52–53, 52

gas masks and respirators **A** (11), 23, **23**, 25
Greek Campaign (1941) 54–55
gunners 26, **C1** (27), 33

Halstead, Michael 10
Hamilton, Stuart 4
handbooks and manuals **G9–10** (59)
headgear
    berets **A** (11), 24
    helmets **A3–5** (11), 23, 24, **24**, 52
    overview 23–24
    sidecaps 24
    sun helmets 30
Hills, Stuart 38, 41, 50–52, 57
hygiene and cleanliness 23, 29, 34, 35, 39, 55

Italian Campaign (1943–45) 32, 44, **F** (51), 56–57, **56**

Jones, Bill 8

Leach, Victor **49**
Leakey, Rea 8, 47–48
leave 38
leisure and entertainment 15, 35–38, **35**, **36**
letters 38
loaders 26, **C3** (27), 33
lorries and trucks 30, 31

maintenance 32, 33, **33**, 34, 36, **D** (37)
medical care **E8** (45), 48, 50, **F** (51), 62
mines **E3** (45), 48, 61
mission 44, 61

Normandy landings and VE Day (1944–45)
    action **E** (45), 57–60
    crew and equipment 21, 35, 57, **G** (58)
    tanks 33, 43, 57
North African Campaign *see* Desert Campaigns

officers 9, 12–14, 16, 41, 62
organization 4–5, 30–32

pay 17
pay books **G8** (59)
petrol cans **A15–16** (11), 34
Powell, John 12

radio operators 26, **C3** (27)
radios 28, **28**, **G5** (59)
Reay, Geordie 12
refuelling 34, **34**
religion 41
Render, David 48
Roberts, Pip 16
Royal Armoured Corps units
    2nd Armoured Brigade 36
    3 RTR 7, 36, 50, 53, 54–55
    4 RTR 25
    5 RTR 10, 53
    6th Guards Tank Brigade 29
    8th Armoured Brigade 33
    8 RTR 40
    40 RTR 31
    44 RTR 53
    50 RTR 39
    146 Regiment 34
    County of London Yeomanry 56
    Fife and Forfar Yeomanry 23, 52

Lancashire Fusiliers 39
Northamptonshire Yeomanry 16
Queen's Own Hussars 42
Royal Hussars 28, 30
Sherwood Rangers Yeomanry 38, 50

Sandhurst 13
scout cars 31
sexual morality 15
Sikh crewmen 13
simulators 9
sleeping 32, 34, 35
stowage 30, 35
submarine escape apparatus **G11** (59)

tank commanders 9, 17, 26–28, **C2** (27), **28**, **29**, 48
tank destroyers **E2** (45)
tank hunter teams **E5** (45)
tank interiors 28–30, **29**
tank transporters 14, **B** (19), 32
tanks
    Churchills 4, 25, 29, 32, 41, 46, 49, **F** (51)
    classes 41
    Comets 43
    Covenanters 41, 48
    Cromwells **C** (27), 46, 57, 58
    Cruisers 32, 40, 43, 53
    Crusaders 12, **B** (19), 35, 48, 55
    DDs 42
    German 5, 40, 42–43, 46, 56
    Grants 33, 34, 42, **42**, 46
    Japanese 61
    Lees **D** (37), 42, 60–61
    Light Tank Mk VIs 30, 52, 54
    Matildas 20, 48, 53, **53**
    picking up new tanks **B** (19)
    Shermans 17, 24, 26, 28, 33, **33**, 40, 42, 43, 44, **E1** (45), 46–47, 49, 56
    Stuarts 41, 60
    Valentines 12, 14, 26, 29, 39, 42, 60
tarpaulins 15, 34
telephones 34, **E7** (45)
Tout, Ken 40, 43, 46
training 8–12, **9**, **12**, 13–14

wading trunks and waterproofing 17, 56
Wardrop, Jake 26, 40
water bottles **A12** (11), 23
Watt, Jock 12, 32
weapons
    anti-tank 49, 57–58, 60, 61
    grenades **A9** (11), 25
    holsters 23, 25, 57
    overview 24–25
    revolvers **A7** (11), 24, 25
    rifles 60
    submachine guns **A8** (11), 25, **G3** (59), 60
    see also armament and gunnery
webbing equipment and braces **A** (11), 20, 23, 24

Yorke, Sergeant 28